MW00643968

Introducing the Second Edition of

Cooking with Chef Brad
Those Wonderful Grains!
Series

Special Features:

- Reformatted cover and layout
- Simplified instructions
- Enhanced recipes using **Those Wonderful Grains!**
- Additional recommended ingredient substitutions
- Additional tips and updated information

Cooking with Chef Brad
Those Wonderful Grains!

Cooking with Chef Brad
Those Wonderful Grains II

Cooking with Chef Brad
Favorite Pressure Cooker Recipes

Cooking with Chef Brad
Whole Grain Comfort Foods

Cooking with Chef Brad

Those Wonderful Grains!

By Brad E Petersen

"Chef Brad"

Second Edition

Grass Valley, California

MemoryMaker Productions
P.O. Box 2524
Grass Valley, CA 95945-2524

Cooking with Chef Brad
Those Wonderful Grains!

First edition published 1999
Second edition published 2011
2011-A-BB
Printed in Hong Kong

ISBN: 978-1-936992-06-5

For questions about ingredients and recipes, check Chef Brad's website:
www.chefbrad.com
or email chef@chefbrad.com

Cover design: Marianne McKnight
Cover photo: Bonnie M. Sorensen and Heather Smith
Chef's hat design: Gloria Armstrong

Acknowledgments

My thanks to the wonderful helpers who sampled and tested every one of these recipes many times over. Special thanks to Marianne McKnight for her careful attention to detail and perfection.

Dedication

To my wife, Louise,
who has given all,
heart, soul, and health,
to let me live my dream.
Words are not enough to express
the feelings I have in my heart
for her.

Table of Contents

Introduction....................1
Quality is Everything....................2
Using the Right Equipment....................2
Resource....................3

Those Wonderful Grains!....................5
Amaranth....................7
Barley, Pearled....................7
Buckwheat....................8
Bulgur Wheat....................8
Couscous....................8
Field Corn....................9
Kamut®....................9
Kasha....................10
Millet....................10
Oats....................11
Popcorn....................12
Quinoa....................12
Rice....................13
Rye....................14
Soybeans....................15
Spelt....................15
Teff....................16
Triticale....................16
Wheat....................17

Recipes....................19
Breads....................19
Pizzas, Bagels, Focaccias, Flat Breads, & Tortillas....................75
Muffins, Pastries, & Pancakes....................91
Cookies, Cakes, & Non-Yeasted Breads....................113
Miscellaneous....................127

Index....................157

Those Wonderful Grains!

Introduction

Friends and family have been encouraging me for years to do a book. I fought back, saying, "I can't!" And I still say "I can't," but here it is anyway—my first book on cooking with grains.

Over the years, especially this past year, I have grown to respect and love the many wonderful grains. I enjoy the different flavors and the unique history that many of the grains have. I have found that knowing about the grains helps me to develop a more personal relationship with them. That in turn helps me to use them more. And the more I use these wonderful grains, the more I enjoy them!

It has been an exciting, though difficult, experience for me to put together this cookbook about grains. The hard part was actually putting down the recipes on paper so that you could cook them. My cooking style is to just throw in anything that sounds good and hope for a great result. I realized, however, that while this works for me, many of you depend on a well-written recipe. I hope you will have as much fun as I have as you venture forth using Those Wonderful Grains! in preparing healthful, delicious food.

The inspiration for many of the recipes in this book falls under the category of "sneak nutrition," a term that I often use. It simply means to sneak nutrition into your family's diet in any way that you can without them knowing about it. I have discovered that using grains is one of the best ways to do this. By simply grinding them and then tossing a little into whatever you are cooking, you increase not only the nutritional value of the food but also the flavor. What a great combination—variety of flavor and quality nutrition! When it comes right down to it, as my grandmother used to say: "The proof is in the pudding." So, use the recipes in this book and see for yourself if cooking with grains is everything that I believe it to be.

Quality is Everything

The most important element in cooking is the quality of the ingredients that is used. I am very particular, especially about the quality of grains I select. It is important to find a reliable source for your grains because using fresh, high quality grains can make the difference in the end result being satisfying or not. I have searched for a long time to find a grains supplier that shares my passion for quality. I finally found that company! I have teamed up with West Mountain Farms from Spanish Fork, Utah, to provide you with the best quality of grains that can be found. We supply flours that are chemical and bromine free. Bromines, chemicals found in most refined flours, are toxic to the human body. Recent research has shown that many people who have a wheat allergy are really fighting the toxins in the grains. That is why I recommend using flours that are bromine free.

Using the Right Equipment

Have you ever tried to do a job without the benefit of the proper tools? Frustrating, isn't it? You can add dramatically to your bread baking and cooking pleasure by using the right equipment in your kitchen.

One of my customers said it well one day when he was shopping for his wife. He said that at work he had access to the best fax machine, cell phone, and computer. This equipment was not cheap. In fact, he noted, he bought only the best to do his job. This wise husband felt it only fair that his wife have high quality equipment to do her job at home.

I discovered that once I started using the proper equipment in the kitchen, I enjoyed cooking more. Not only was I more satisfied with the finished product, I also found that the journey to achieving those wondrous results was fun and exciting.

There are many gadgets that I enjoy using in the kitchen, but the two pieces of equipment I would never do without are my Bosch mixer and a good grain mill.

Bosch Mixer:

Baking bread without a Bosch is like trying to mow the grass with a push mower. Yes, the push mower gets the job done, but who looks forward to mowing the grass knowing the extra work involved? There are other food processors or dough makers on the market, but the serious bread maker knows that the Bosch is really the only machine to have. It has a long history of dependability and holds up under the heavy demands of family use with little, if any, need for repair. Packed with power, the Bosch takes bread making to a whole new dimension.

From start to finish, I can bake six loaves of bread in a little over an hour. It is amazing. Just how does the Bosch mixer work? The basic principle of the Bosch is the design teamed up with power. The design of the machine and bowl allows for easy mixing, and the power develops the gluten in minutes. In fact, six minutes of mixing in the Bosch is equivalent to two bread risings. I love my Bosch!

Grain Mill:

Another must for the serious bread maker is a good mill. I recommend one that is quiet and easy to clean. A grain mill is one of the best investments for health and nutrition if you are going to start using whole grains. Nothing can compare to the ease of grinding grains right in your own kitchen, not to overlook the tremendous health benefits derived from freshly ground grains.

Resource

For the latest information about products and ingredients for your kitchen, go to www.chefbrad.com. If you have questions about specific recipes or ingredients, email me at chef@chefbrad.com.

Those Wonderful Grains!

Amaranth

One of the super grains, amaranth has a wonderful history. Native to the Americas, it has been used in South America for centuries. Amaranth was one of the staples in the ancient Aztec culture and was an important part of their ceremonies. Montezuma used this grain to tax his people.

Amaranth is a very prolific weed. One plant can contain as many as one million seeds. Amaranth has a very low gluten content and stores well. It has superior nutritional value; it contains high-quality protein, fiber, iron, and vitamin C and is lysine rich. The green leaves, best boiled like kale, are powerhouses of potassium and vitamin A. Cook amaranth with other grains to increase its protein value.

Amaranth Popping Instructions: One of the most wonderful things about this grain is that it can be popped. By placing about two tablespoons of the grain in a deep, dry, hot pan, it pops very quickly. One-fourth cup of the grain will yield 1 cup of popped amaranth. Add this popped grain to dough to lighten its texture.

Use amaranth as a flour—whole or popped—in breads, cookies, pastries, soups, and salads.

Nutrient content per 1/2 cup amaranth:

364 calories	148 mg calcium	7 g dietary fiber	1.3 mg niacin
14 g protein	443 mg phosph.	0 RE vit. A	356 mg potassium
6 g fat	7.4 mg iron	.08 mg thiamin	65 g carbohydrate
1 g sat. fat	21 mg sodium	.20 mg riboflavin	
0 mg cholesterol		4 mg vitamin C	

Barley, Pearled

Used long before wheat ever was, barley is believed to be the world's oldest cultivated grain.

Pearled barley has part or all of the germ and bran removed and has a substance that inhibits cholesterol formation. Whole barley has only the outer husk removed and is high in protein, potassium, fiber, and calcium. Barley flakes are also high in fiber. Remember, the finer the barley, the more it has been milled and the fewer nutrients it will have.

The bread made from barley is probably heavy since barley contains only small amounts of gluten. Perhaps the most common use of barley is for making such alcoholic beverages as Scotch whiskey and beer, which cannot be made without it. Animal fodder is also made from barley.

Use barley in breads, soups, pilafs, and salads.

Nutrient content per 1/2 cup cooked pearl barley:

193 calories	17 mg calcium	9 g dietary fiber	0 mg vitamin C
4 g protein	85 mg phosph.	1 RE vitamin A	3.2 mg niacin
1 g fat, 0 sat.fat	2.1 mg iron	.13 mg thiamin	146 mg potassium
0 mg cholesterol	5 mg sodium	.10 mg riboflavin	44 g carbohydrate

Buckwheat

A native of Russia, buckwheat is another of the super grains. It is not an actual grain, however, but an herb—and a very flexible one. Flour made from buckwheat seed is used to make pancakes in the United States, pasta in Italy, soba (pasta) in Japan, and kasha in Russia. High in all eight essential amino acids, gluten-free buckwheat is high in calcium and vitamins E and B.

Use buckwheat in breads, side dishes, cereals, pancakes, and salads.

Bulgur Wheat

With a long history in Asia, bulgur wheat is steamed wheat kernels that have been dried and crushed. Though the two are often confused, bulgur wheat is not exactly the same as cracked wheat.

Because of the limited fuel in some parts of the world, bulgur wheat is used often because it cooks up very quickly, having already been steamed. It is rich in bran and germ.

Use bulgur wheat in salads, breakfast cereal, and breads.

Couscous

Although couscous is not a grain, it can be used like one. Very flexible, couscous—the Arabic word for "semolina"—stores well, cooks quickly, and can be seasoned in many ways.

Couscous is refined durum wheat flour that has been rolled into thin strands, crumbled into little pieces, steamed, and dried.

In the United States couscous is used as a substitute for rice, potatoes, and even pasta. Also use couscous in side dishes.

Nutrient content of 1 cup boiled couscous:

201 calories	15 mg calcium	5 g dietary fiber	0 mg vitamin C
7 g protein	39 mg phosph.	0 RE vitamin A	1.8 mg niacin
0 g fat, 0 sat.fat	.7 mg iron	.11 mg thiamin	104 mg potassium
0 mg cholesterol	9 mg sodium	.05 mg riboflavin	42 g carbohydrate

Field Corn

Corn, or maize as it is known in most places around the world, was originally the generic term for any grain in Europe. Though maize was being grown in China and the Philippines about the sixteenth century, it was essentially developed and cultivated by the Indian civilizations in both North and South America. The Andean and Mexican cultures as well as North America's Native Americans worshipped maize as a crucial crop of survival. In the lore of these civilizations is found references to corn as the "Seed of Seeds," "Sacred Mother," or "Gift of the Gods."

Field corn, or dent corn, is usually dried right in the fields, creating a dent at the top of the kernel, hence its alternate name. Yellow, white, red, or blue kernels can be eaten fresh, dried, cracked, or ground into a variety of products. Use field corn in corn tortillas, corn breads, mush, breads, and cereals.

Kamut®

One of the most wonderful of all grains, Kamut® comes from the ancient Egyptian word for "wheat." This grain was a staple in the Egyptian lifestyle and was probably one of the grains that Joseph stored for the Pharaoh. Kamut® was rediscovered about 1950 by a farmer from Montana who brought home a handful of kernels from Egypt and planted them on his farm.

Kamut® has a rich, deliciously buttery flavor and chewy texture. It is wonderful to use in breads and pancakes. It does contain gluten but many wheat-sensitive eat it without any reaction.

Its kernels are two to three times larger than wheat, thirty percent higher in protein, and richer in magnesium, zinc, and vitamin E.

Kamut® flakes, similar to oatmeal, are made by heating whole grains and then pressing them flat.

Use Kamut® flour in pancakes, cookies, and pastries. Use whole grain Kamut® in salads, soups, and side dishes.

Nutrient content per 1 cup cooked Kamut®:

258 calories	18 mg sodium
10 g protein	4 g dietary fiber
3 g fat	44 g carbohydrate

Kasha

Gluten-free kasha is perfect for those with wheat allergies. In the United States, kasha refers to roasted buckwheat groats. It has a strong, nutty aroma and toasty flavor.

Use kasha in salads, soups, breads, side dishes, pancakes, and waffles.

Nutrient content per 1 cup cooked kasha (roasted buckwheat):

182 calories	138 mg phosph.	1.6 mg iron	.08 mg riboflavin
7 g protein	39 g carbohydrate	8 mg sodium	1.9 mg niacin
1 g fat, 0 sat.	14 mg calcium	174 mg potassium	0 mg vitamin C
0 mg cholesterol	5 g dietary fiber	.08 mg thiamin	0 RE vitamin A

Millet

One of the super grains, gluten-free millet is one of the most versatile and nutritious of all grains. It is very rich in amino acids, phosphorus, and vitamin B as well as lysine, a high-quality protein vitamin. Its iron content is higher than any grain except for amaranth and quinoa.

Although in America it is primarily used as birdseed and fodder, millet is a staple for almost one-third of the world's population, particularly in disadvantaged regions of Asia and Africa.

Millet is easy to digest and is one of the most outstanding alkaline foods in the world. Soothing to people on diets, it is recommended for those suffering from ulcers and colitis.

Millet has a bland flavor but if toasted before boiled, tastes similar to hot buttered popcorn. Millet makes a great meat substitute in soups and beans.

Use millet in cereals, breads, soups, salads, and side dishes.

Nutrient content per 1 cup boiled millet:

284 calories	7 mg calcium	3 g dietary fiber	0 mg vitamin C
8 g protein	240 mg phosph.	0 RE vitamin A	3.2 mg niacin
2 g fat, 0 sat.fat	1.5 mg iron	.25 mg thiamin	149 mg potassium
0 mg cholesterol	5 mg sodium	.20 mg riboflavin	57 g carbohydrate

Oats

Oats have excellent nutritional qualities and are rich in high-quality protein, seven B vitamins, calcium, fiber, and unsaturated fats. Flour from oats is gluten free, and it is believed that oat bran lowers cholesterol.

The reason oatmeal keeps longer than other grains is because the heat used to process it destroys the enzymes that hasten staling. Oat groats are untreated, natural, hulled oats with the outermost inedible chaff or hull removed. Quick oats are groats that have been steel-cut into pieces before being steamed and flattened by steel rollers into thin flakes. Quick oats have less texture and are less chewy than rolled oats.

Steaming then crushing oat groats between steel rollers make rolled oats, also called old-fashioned oats. The cholesterol-lowering bran and B vitamins are retained. Old-fashioned groats and quick oats can usually be interchanged in recipes.

Use oats in cereal, cookies, breads, pancakes, and waffles.

Nutrient content per 1 cup cooked oat bran:

88 calories	22 mg calcium	7 g dietary fiber	0 mg vitamin C
7 g protein	261 mg phosph.	0 RE vitamin A	.3 mg niacin
2 g fat, 0 sat.fat	1.9 mg iron	.35 mg thiamin	201 mg potassium
0 mg cholesterol	2 mg sodium	.07 mg riboflavin	25 g carbohydrate

Nutrient content per 1 cup cooked oatmeal:

145 calories	19 mg calcium	5 g dietary fiber	0 mg vitamin C
6 g protein	177 mg phosph.	5 RE vitamin A	.3 mg niacin
2 g fat, 0 sat.fat	1.6 mg iron	.26 mg thiamin	131 mg potassium
0 mg cholesterol	2 mg sodium	.05 mg riboflavin	25 g carbohydrate

Popcorn

Popcorn is the all-American snack and probably one of the most healthful—if it is not popped in oil, drenched in butter, or sprinkled with salt. It is full of dietary fiber, low in calories, and free of saturated fat.

Popcorn is one of the ancient grains, said to date back at least six thousand years. The Incas are known to have used strings of popcorn for their ceremonies. The early settlers popped it as the first breakfast cereal.

What makes popcorn unique is that it contains a very hard hull and about thirteen percent internal moisture. With nowhere to go when the kernel is heated, the moisture becomes steam and ...popcorn!

Popcorn comes in many styles—white, yellow, red, blue, plain, flavored, oil-popped, and air-popped, to name a few. It contains less starch than field corn and makes the best corn bread ever.

Use popcorn in corn bread, breads, dusting flour, pancakes, and waffles.

Nutrient content per 1 cup popcorn (air-popped, unsalted, and unbuttered):

31 calories	1 mg calcium	1 g dietary fiber	0 mg vitamin C
1 g protein	24 mg phosph.	2 RE vitamin A	.2 mg niacin
0 g fat, 0 sat.fat	.2 mg iron	.02 mg thiamin	24 mg potassium
0 mg cholesterol	0 mg sodium	.02 mg riboflavin	6 g carbohydrate

Quinoa (Red, Black, and White)

Quinoa is another one of the super grains. It contains more protein than any other grain. In fact, it is considered a complete protein since it contains all eight essential amino acids.

Quinoa is also high in unsaturated fats and lower in carbohydrates than most grains. It is loaded with phosphorus, niacin, iron, and potassium, and is high in lysine. Quinoa will expand to four times its original volume.

The staple of the ancient Incan civilization, quinoa was called the "Mother Grain." When planting this highly revered grain, the Inca Indians used a solid gold shovel. Quinoa is still used as a staple in South America.

Use quinoa in side dishes, pancakes, soups, cereals, breads, and waffles.

Nutrient content per 1/2 cup dry quinoa:

318 calories	51 mg calcium	4 g dietary fiber	0 mg vitamin C
11 g protein	349 mg phosph.	0 RE vitamin A	2.5 mg niacin
5 g fat, 1 sat.fat	7.9 mg iron	.17 mg thiamin	629 mg potassium
0 mg cholesterol	18 mg sodium	.34 mg riboflavin	59 g carbohydrate

Rice

The traditional bowl of rice is by far the most important food in the world today. Half the world's population eats it three times a day.

Rice is one of the most nutritious of grains, low in fat and sodium and high in fiber. It is composed of about eighty percent carbohydrates and contains small amounts of protein, vitamin B1, phosphorus, and potassium.

Brown rice is more nutritious than white, which is primarily starch. It retains its oil-rich germ and bran and is packed with vitamins. It also contains fiber and protein. Basmati rice is a long-grain, aromatic variety. To develop its full flavor, this rice is aged for at least a year after harvest. It doubles its length while cooking. All types of rice are high-carbohydrate, low-fat, low-sodium food that supplies iron and many of the B vitamins.

Use rice in breads, cereals, side dishes, and soups.

Nutrient content per 1 cup cooked long-grain white rice:

267 calories	21 mg calcium	1 g dietary fiber	0 mg vitamin C
6 g protein	88 mg phosph.	0 RE vitamin A	3 mg niacin
1 g fat, 0 sat.fat	2.5 mg iron	.33 mg thiamin	72 mg potassium
0 mg cholesterol	2 mg sodium	.03 mg riboflavin	58 g carbohydrate

Nutrient content per 1 cup long-grain brown rice:

216 calories	20 mg calcium	3 g dietary fiber	0 mg vitamin C
5 g protein	161 mg phosph.	0 RE vitamin A	3 mg niacin
2 g fat, 0 sat.fat	.8 mg iron	.19 mg thiamin	84 mg potassium
0 mg cholesterol	10 mg sodium	.05 mg riboflavin	45 g carbohydrate

Rye

This grain gets a bad rap because of the flavor of the caraway seed used in rye breads. Rye alone is not very flavorful, hence the need to add caraway seeds and molasses to the recipes.

The other misconception is that rye bread is made with all-rye flour. Actually, only about one-third of the total flour in most rye bread is rye flour.

Low in gluten, rye is high in lysine, fiber, protein, phosphorus, iron, and potassium. It has a special long chain of five-carbon sugars, which digest slowly, imparting a sense of fullness.

Rye has the ability to grow in poor soil, in harsh climates, and at high altitudes. It is called "the grain of poverty," as it sustained the poor of Germany, Poland, Russia, and Scandinavia.

Use rye in breads, pastries, cookies, pancakes, and waffles.

Nutrient content per 1/2 cup cooked rye:

98 calories	0 mg sodium
4 g protein	2 g dietary fiber
0 g fat	24 g carbohydrate

Soybeans

One of the earth's oldest and most valuable crops, soybeans are the richest plant food known to man.

Highly important in the Chinese culture, soybeans are considered one of the five sacred grains—along with rice, wheat, barley, and millet. Low in carbohydrates and high in protein, soybeans are used to produce a wide variety of products, including tofu, soybean oil, soy flour, soy milk, soy sauce, miso, and tamari. No part of the soybean plant is ever wasted.

Soybeans are the principal ingredient in Textured Vegetable Protein, now being used in meatless burgers.

Use soybeans in breads.

Nutrient content per 1 cup cooked fresh soybeans:

254 calories	262 mg calcium	4 g dietary fiber	31 mg vitamin C
22 g protein	284 mg phosph.	29 RE vitamin A	2.3 mg niacin
12 g fat, 1 sat. fat	4.5 mg iron	.47 mg thiamin	970 mg potassium
0 mg cholesterol	25 mg sodium	.28 mg riboflavin	20 g carbohydrate

Spelt

A super grain in its own right, nothing can be said bad about spelt except its cost. Because it has to be harvested differently than wheat and the yield is so much smaller, the price is high. For wheat-intolerant people, however, it is well worth the cost.

Spelt is a true non-hybrid grain, and spelt flour can be easily substituted for wheat flour in baked goods. Spelt contains the eight essential amino acids. It is about sixty percent higher in protein than wheat and contains B vitamins, iron, potassium, magnesium, and fiber.

This grain with the deliciously light, nutty flavor has been grown and eaten around the world for the last five thousand years.

Use spelt in anything in which wheat flour is used—and more.

Nutrient content per 1/2 cup cooked spelt:
100 calories 1 g fat
4 g protein 3.5 g dietary fiber
0 mg sodium
26 g carbohydrate

Teff

Yet another of the super grains, gluten-free teff is one of the nutritious giants. It is much higher in iron and calcium than wheat, rice, millet, or oats. It is also a rich source of other minerals, including magnesium, boron, copper, phosphorus, and zinc.

Teff is the smallest grain in the world, so tiny it takes a hundred fifty teff seeds to equal the weight of a single wheat kernel. Because it is so tiny, the entire grain must be milled for there is no way to remove the germ or the husk. Teff has been the "rice and wheat" of Ethiopia for centuries

Teff now comes in three colors—red, brown, and white. White is the most delicate and the mildest of the three. Even though it is white, it is not processed. The red and brown teff have a richer, nuttier flavor. Teff is used to boost nutritional value in such foods as meat loaves and muffins.

Use teff in salads, side dishes, cookies, cakes, muffins, pancakes, waffles, and breads.

Nutrient content per 2-oz. serving of teff:
200 calories 1 g fat
7 g protein 250 mg potassium
10 mg sodium
41 g carbohydrate

Triticale

The first human-engineered grain in history, triticale is a high-protein rye-wheat hybrid. It is low in gluten and high in lysine, protein, and some B vitamins.

This grain can be used much the same way as soft wheat. Products made with triticale flour are very tender, and their flavor, texture, crust, and crumb color are similar to those of products containing wheat.

Triticale flakes are made by heating whole triticale until soft and then pressing flat with steel rollers.

Use triticale in soups, cakes, breads, pancakes, and waffles.

Nutrient content per 1 cup triticale flour:

439 calories	46 mg calcium	19 g dietary fiber	0 mg vitamin C
17 g protein	417 mg phosph.	0 RE vitamin A	3.7 mg niacin
2 g fat, 0 sat.fat	3.4 mg iron	.49 mg thiamin	605 mg potassium
0 mg cholesterol	3 mg sodium	.17 mg riboflavin	95 g carbohydrate

Nutrient content per 1/2 cup cooked triticale:

129 calories	4 g fat	4 g dietary fiber
5 g protein	1.5 mg sodium	
0 mg cholesterol	27 g carbohydrate	

Wheat (Red, White, and Soft)

It is not known when this grain originated, but it is thought to have been ten to fifteen thousand years BC. Considered by most Americans as "the staff of life," wheat is grown in every country in the world and all over the United States.

Wheat contains thirteen B vitamins, vitamin E, protein, essential fatty acids, and important trace minerals. It also contains high amounts of gluten, the protein that provides the elasticity necessary for excellent bread making.

There are four major types of wheat available today—hard red, hard white, soft, and durum. Hard red wheat is high in protein (ten to fourteen percent) and can be sprouted. Although it is great for bread making, it is heavy and, as an acid-based grain, causes many people digestive problems. Hard white wheat is also high in protein. A cross between hard red wheat and soft white wheat, it retains the good qualities of both. Since it is an alkaline-based grain, hard white wheat is easier for most people to digest. It makes a very light loaf of bread.

Soft wheat is low in protein and low in gluten (six to ten percent). Soft wheat is used in making biscuits, cakes, pastries, cookies, and pancakes. Durum wheat, the hardest wheat, is high in gluten and protein. Its hard starch granules hold pasta together in boiling water. Durum wheat is used for pastas and noodles.

Cracked wheat is whole wheat berries that have been cracked into small pieces between steel rollers, which reduces cooking time. Cracked wheat contains all the nutrients of the whole grain. Wheat flakes are steam-pressed wheat berries.

Nutrient content per 1 cup cooked wheat:

84 calories	9 mg calcium	3 g dietary fiber	0 mg vitamin C
4 g protein	78 mg phosph.	0 RE vitamin A	1.5 mg niacin
<1 g fat, 0 sat.fat	.9 mg iron	.12 mg thiamin	99 mg potassium
0 mg cholesterol	1 mg sodium	.03 mg riboflavin	20 g carbohydrate

Breads

Basic Whole Wheat Bread

This is a wonderful basic whole wheat bread recipe. The secret is the hard white wheat flour and the high gluten bread flour. You can choose to omit the high gluten bread flour, but I like the little extra boost it gives.

- 6 c. hot water (110 degrees)
- 10 c. hard white wheat flour
- 2 Tbsp. salt
- 2/3 c. oil
- 2/3 c. honey
- 3 Tbsp. dough enhancer
- 6–8 c. high gluten bread flour
- 3 Tbsp. Saf-Instant® or other instant yeast

Preheat oven to 400 degrees. Combine ingredients in Bosch bowl with dough hook, using only half of the flour, placing flour in last with yeast on top. Begin mixing, adding enough remaining flour until dough cleans sides of bowl (it may not require all of the flour). Knead 6 minutes or until gluten has developed. Remove from bowl and divide into loaves. Form loaves for pans or freestanding loaves. Let rise to double. Bake in preheated oven, dropping temperature to 325 degrees. Bake 20–25 minutes or until internal bread temperature reaches 180 degrees.

Yield: 5 loaves

Chef Brad tip

Using a bread thermometer helps in deciding when bread is done. When the temperature reads 180 degrees, the bread is ready to take out of the oven.

Good Ol' White Bread

Yum yum! My mother made the best white bread ever—light, fluffy, and what wonderful toast! It wasn't packed with nutrition but, oh ,what a treat!

6 c. hot water (110 degrees)
3/4 c. butter
3/4 c. sugar
2 Tbsp. salt
16–18 c. high gluten bread flour
3 Tbsp. Saf-Instant® or other instant yeast

Preheat oven to 400 degrees. Combine ingredients in Bosch bowl with dough hook, using only half of the flour, placing flour in last with yeast on top. Begin mixing, adding enough remaining flour until dough cleans sides of bowl (it may not require all of the flour). Knead 6 minutes or until gluten has developed. Remove from bowl and divide into loaves. Form loaves for pans or freestanding loaves. Let rise to double. Bake in preheated oven, dropping temperature to 325 degrees. Bake 20–25 minutes or until internal bread temperature reaches 180 degrees.

Yield: 5 loaves

Cranberry Vanilla Seed Bread

Makes extra special toast! This is my first recipe to create. I am so proud! It's one of the best breads. You will love it!

- 6 c. water
- 2/3 c. canola oil
- 2/3 c. honey
- 2 Tbsp. vanilla extract
- 2 Tbsp. salt
- 3 c. Cranberry Seed Mixture
- 6–8 c. high gluten bread flour
- 10 c. hard white wheat, flour, freshly ground
- 3 Tbsp. Saf-Instant® or other instant yeast

Preheat oven to 400 degrees. Combine ingredients in Bosch bowl with dough hook, using only half of the flour, placing flour in last with yeast on top. Begin mixing, adding enough remaining flour until dough cleans sides of bowl (it may not require all of the flour). Knead 6 minutes or until gluten has developed. Remove from bowl and divide into loaves. Form loaves for pans or freestanding loaves. Let rise to double. Bake in preheated oven, dropping temperature to 325 degrees. Bake 20–25 minutes or until internal bread temperature reaches 180 degrees.

Yield: 5 loaves

Cranberry Seed Mixture:

- 2 c. sunflower seeds
- 2 c. pumpkin seeds
- 2 c. sesame seeds
- 3 c. almonds, slivered
- 2 c. cranberries, dried
- 1 c. flax seeds
- 1 c. coconut

Grandma's Rye Bread

Old recipe, hence the bacon grease. This bread is heavy but wonderful.

- 6 c. hot water (110 degrees)
- 1/2 c. sugar
- 1/2 c. bacon grease or butter
- 2 Tbsp. salt
- 3 Tbsp. molasses
- 2 Tbsp. dough enhancer
- 6–8 c. rye flour
- 10 c. high gluten bread flour
- 1 Tbsp. caraway seeds (optional)
- 3 Tbsp. Saf-Instant® or other instant yeast

Preheat oven to 400 degrees. Combine ingredients in Bosch bowl with dough hook, using only half of the flour, placing flour in last with yeast on top. Begin mixing, adding enough remaining flour until dough cleans sides of bowl (it may not require all of the flour). Knead 6 minutes or until gluten has developed. Remove from bowl and divide into loaves. Form loaves for pans or freestanding loaves. Let rise to double. Bake in preheated oven, dropping temperature to 325 degrees. Bake 20–25 minutes or until internal bread temperature reaches 180 degrees.

Variation:

Try with spelt flour instead of high gluten flour.

Yield: 5 loaves

Chef Brad tip

If you don't like rye bread, try baking it without the caraway seeds. To some people, including me, caraway tastes like bug spray.

Breakfast Bread

- 6 c. hot water (110 degrees)
- 2/3 c. honey
- 3 Tbsp. cinnamon
- 2 c. currants
- 2 Tbsp. salt
- 2 c. high gluten bread flour
- 2 c. sunflower seeds
- 4 Tbsp. dough enhancer
- 12–16 c. hard white wheat, flour
- 2/3 c. canola oil
- 4 Tbsp. Saf-Instant® or other instant yeast

Preheat oven to 400 degrees. Combine ingredients in Bosch bowl with dough hook, using only half of the flour, placing flour in last with yeast on top. Begin mixing, adding enough remaining flour until dough cleans sides of bowl (it may not require all of the flour). Knead 6 minutes or until gluten has developed. Remove from bowl and divide into loaves. Form loaves for pans or freestanding loaves. Let rise to double. Bake in preheated oven, dropping temperature to 325 degrees. Bake 20–25 minutes or until internal bread temperature reaches 180 degrees.

Yield: 5 loaves

Buttermilk Bread

- 1 c. very hot water
- 1/4 c. honey
- 1-1/4 c. cold buttermilk
- 2 tsp. salt
- 4 Tbsp. butter, chopped in chunks
- 2 c. pastry flour or soft white wheat flour
- 4–6 c. hard white wheat flour
- 1 Tbsp. Saf-Instant® or other instant yeast

Preheat oven to 400 degrees. Combine ingredients in Bosch bowl with dough hook, using only half of the flour, placing flour in last with yeast on top. Begin mixing, adding enough remaining flour until dough cleans sides of bowl (it may not require all of the flour). Knead 6 minutes or until gluten has developed. Remove from bowl and divide into loaves. Form loaves for pans or freestanding loaves. Let rise to double. Bake in preheated oven, dropping temperature to 325 degrees. Bake 20–25 minutes or until internal bread temperature reaches 180 degrees.

Yield: 2 loaves

Chef Brad tip

The stickier the dough, the lighter the roll.

California Walnut Bread

Wonderful nutty bread! I like to bake this one freestanding on a pizza stone.

Sponge:

- 1/4 c. hot water (110 degrees)
- 2 c. high gluten bread flour
- 2 c. warm milk
- 3 Tbsp. sugar
- 2 Tbsp. Saf-Instant® or other instant yeast

Prepare sponge by mixing ingredients together and letting set until bubbly, about one hour.

Dough:

- 1-1/2 c. walnuts, toasted
- 1/2 c. walnut oil
- 1 Tbsp. salt
- 3–4 c. high gluten bread flour
- Sponge

Preheat oven to 400 degrees. In Bosch bowl with dough hook add dough ingredients to sponge, using only half the high gluten flour. Begin mixing, adding flour until dough cleans sides of bowl. Knead for 6 minutes to develop gluten. Divide into 3 free-standing loaves and let rise until double in size. After placing bread in oven, drop temperature to 325 degrees. Bake 20–25 minutes or until internal bread temperature reaches 180 degrees.

Yield: 3 loaves

Chef Brad tip

Roasting nuts brings out the natural oils which enhance the flavor.

Cracked Wheat Feather Bread

A great way to use leftover cereal! Texture-perfect bread if you like a little crunch.

- 2 c. boiling water
- 2 c. cracked wheat
- 2 c. popping corn
- 1 c. whole oat groats
- 4 c. hot water (110 degrees)
- 3/4 c. shortening
- 1 c. sugar
- 2 Tbsp. salt
- 2 Tbsp. dough enhancer
- 10–12 c. high gluten bread flour
- 3 Tbsp. Saf-Instant® or other instant yeast

Preheat oven to 400 degrees. Place cracked wheat into 2 cups boiling water and let sit for 10 minutes. Grind popping corn and whole oat groats. Set aside. Place hot water in Bosch bowl with dough hook with cracked wheat/boiling water. Add shortening and mix to dissolve shortening. Add sugar, salt, dough enhancer, ground popping corn, and oat groats. Add about 6 cups flour, placing yeast on top. Begin mixing, adding flour until dough cleans sides of bowl. Knead for 6 minutes to develop gluten. Remove from bowl and divide into loaves. Form loaves for pans or freestanding loaves. Let rise to double. Bake in preheated oven, dropping temperature to 325 degrees. Bake 20–25 minutes or until internal bread temperature reaches 180 degrees.

Yield: 5 loaves

Wild Rice Molasses Bread

- 1-1/4 c. hot water (110 degrees)
- 1 c. warm milk
- 1/2 c. walnut oil
- 1/2 c. molasses
- 1-1/2 c. cooked wild rice
- Pinch brown sugar
- 2-1/2 tsp. salt
- 2-1/2 c. hard white wheat flour
- 2 Tbsp. Saf-Instant® or other instant yeast
- 4-1/2 c. (approx.) high gluten bread flour

Preheat oven to 400 degrees. Combine ingredients in Bosch bowl with dough hook, using only half of the flour, placing flour in last with yeast on top. Begin mixing, adding enough remaining flour until dough cleans sides of bowl (it may not require all of the flour). Knead 6 minutes or until gluten has developed. Remove from bowl and divide into loaves. Form two round loaves. Let rise to double. Bake in preheated oven, dropping temperature to 325 degrees. Bake 20–25 minutes or until internal bread temperature reaches 180 degrees. For a different looking bread, try baking as freestanding loaves on pizza stone.

Yield: 2 loaves

Chef Brad tip

This whole grain loaf is richly flavored and lightly textured yet chewy and as soul-satisfying as good bread gets. Add flour judiciously to keep the dough very soft.

Buttermilk Multi-Grain Bread

2 c. hot fresh buttermilk, (110 degrees)
4 Tbsp. butter
2 tsp. salt
1/3 c. barley malt syrup
1 Tbsp. dough enhancer
1 c. 9-grain cracked cereal mix
2 c. white wheat flour, freshly ground
2–4 c. high gluten bread flour
1 Tbsp. Saf-Instant® or other instant yeast

Preheat oven to 400 degrees. Combine ingredients in Bosch bowl with dough hook, using only half of the flour, placing flour in last with yeast on top. Begin mixing, adding enough remaining flour until dough cleans sides of bowl (it may not require all of the flour). Knead 6 minutes or until gluten has developed. Remove from bowl and divide into loaves. Form loaves for pans or freestanding loaves. Let rise to double. Bake in preheated oven, dropping temperature to 325 degrees. Bake 20–25 minutes or until internal bread temperature reaches 180 degrees.

Yield: 2 loaves

Chef Brad tip

Soybeans act as a dough enhancer. Try grinding up 1/4 cup to 8 cups of flour and adding it to your dough.

Vienna Bread

- 1 egg
- 2 Tbsp. oil
- 1 Tbsp. honey
- 2 tsp. salt
- 2-1/2 c. hot water (110 degrees)
- 6 c. whole wheat or spelt flour
- 1 Tbsp. Saf-Instant® or other instant yeast

Preheat oven to 400 degrees. Combine ingredients in Bosch bowl with dough hook, using only half of the flour, placing flour in last with yeast on top. Begin mixing, adding enough remaining flour until dough cleans sides of bowl (it may not require all of the flour). Knead 6 minutes or until gluten has developed. Remove from bowl and divide into loaves. Form loaves for pans or freestanding loaves. Let rise to double. Bake in preheated oven, dropping temperature to 325 degrees.

This bread must be steamed while baking to ensure a great crust. While bread is baking, brush or spray bread with water every 3 minutes until the bread starts to brown. Closing oven quickly will prevent heat loss. This method works best when baking on a pizza stone, as the stone holds the oven's heat. Bake 20–25 minutes or until internal temperature reaches 180 degrees.

Yield: 2 loaves

Raisin Rye Bread

One of the most popular and "toothsome" rye breads! This is a mildly sweet, all-occasion bread that makes outstanding rolls as well.

- 1 c. raisins
- 1 c. water
- 3 Tbsp. molasses
- 1 tsp. salt
- 2 c. rye flour
- 2–3 c. hard white wheat flour
- 2 Tbsp. cider vinegar
- 1/2 tsp. caraway seeds
- 2 Tbsp. oil
- 1 c. water (plus raisin water)
- 2 tsp. Saf-Instant® or other instant yeast

Preheat oven to 400 degrees. Boil raisins in 1 cup water for 5 minutes. Combine ingredients in Bosch bowl with dough hook, using only half of the flour, placing flour in last with yeast on top. Begin mixing, adding enough remaining flour until dough cleans sides of bowl (it may not require all of the flour). Knead 6 minutes or until gluten has developed. Remove from bowl and divide into loaves. Form loaves for pans or freestanding loaves. Let rise to double. Bake in preheated oven, dropping temperature to 325 degrees. Bake 20–25 minutes or until internal bread temperature reaches 180 degrees.

Yield: 2 loaves

Lemony Fennelly Bread

The lemon and fennel combination makes a delicate, buttery, light, and tender loaf.

3 c. high gluten bread flour
3–5 c. hard white wheat flour
3 c. hot water (110 degrees)
1-1/2 tsp. fennel seed
2-1/2 tsp. salt
4 Tbsp. butter
1/4 c. honey
1 Tbsp. lemon peel, freshly grated
Juice of 1 lemon
2/3 c .buttermilk powder
3 Tbsp. Saf-Instant® or other instant yeast

Preheat oven to 400 degrees. Combine ingredients in Bosch bowl with dough hook, using only half of the flour, placing flour in last with yeast on top. Begin mixing, adding enough remaining flour until dough cleans sides of bowl (it may not require all of the flour). Knead 6 minutes or until gluten has developed. Remove from bowl and divide into loaves. Form loaves for pans or freestanding loaves. Let rise to double. Bake in preheated oven, dropping temperature to 325 degrees. Bake 20–25 minutes or until internal bread temperature reaches 180 degrees.

Yield: 3 loaves

Herb Bread

This is a great bread for dipping in sauce and oil.

- 4 c. hot water (110 degrees)
- 1 c. buttermilk (110 degrees)
- 1/4 c. safflower oil
- 1/4 c. honey
- 2 tsp. salt
- 14–17 c. hard white wheat flour
- 2 Tbsp. garlic, minced
- 1/4 c. onion, dried
- 2 Tbsp. dill
- 2 Tbsp. oregano
- 1 Tbsp. rosemary
- 2 Tbsp. Saf-Instant® or other instant yeast

Preheat oven to 400 degrees. Combine ingredients in Bosch bowl with dough hook, using only half of the flour, placing flour in last with yeast on top. Begin mixing, adding enough remaining flour until dough cleans sides of bowl (it may not require all of the flour). Knead 6 minutes or until gluten has developed. Remove from bowl and divide into loaves. Form loaves for pans or freestanding loaves. Let rise to double. Bake in preheated oven, dropping temperature to 325 degrees. Bake 20–25 minutes or until internal bread temperature reaches 180 degrees.

Yield: 5 loaves

Chef Brad tip

For a real treat, try mixing olive oil, balsamic vinegar, and plum vinegar to dip bread in.

Potato Bread

My family calls this bread "cake." It's soft, chewy, and light as a feather. Don't turn your back on this one; it will disappear!

- 2 large potatoes, peeled and cooked
- 1/2 c. butter (1 stick)
- 6 c. hot water (110 degrees)
- 3/4 c. sugar
- 2 Tbsp. salt
- 16–18 c. high gluten bread flour
- 3 Tbsp. Saf-Instant® or other instant yeast

Preheat oven to 400 degrees. Combine ingredients in Bosch bowl with dough hook, using only half of the flour, placing flour in last with yeast on top. Begin mixing, adding enough remaining flour until dough cleans sides of bowl (it may not require all of the flour). Knead 6 minutes or until gluten has developed. Remove from bowl and divide into loaves. Form loaves for pans or freestanding loaves. Let rise to double. Bake in preheated oven, dropping temperature to 325 degrees. Bake 20–25 minutes or until internal bread temperature reaches 180 degrees.

Yield: 6 loaves

Chef Brad tip

You can use any of the grains you want in any of these recipes as long as you don't exceed more than a third of the total flour with the non-wheat flour.

Black Bean Jalapeño Bread

A great bread! Just a tint of spice. Makes the most wonderful toasted cheese sandwiches.

- 3 c. hot water (110 degrees)
- 1/3 c. butter, melted
- 1 c. sourdough starter
- 1/2 c. diced jalapeño peppers
- 1/2 can whole kernel corn, drained
- 1/3 c. sugar
- 1/2 c. black dry bean flour
- 9–11 c. high gluten bread flour
- 2 Tbsp. Saf-Instant® or other instant yeast

Preheat oven to 400 degrees. Combine ingredients in Bosch bowl with dough hook, using only half of the flour, placing flour in last with yeast on top. Begin mixing, adding enough remaining flour until dough cleans sides of bowl (it may not require all of the flour). Knead 6 minutes or until gluten has developed. Remove from bowl and divide into loaves. Form loaves for pans or freestanding loaves. Let rise to double. Bake in preheated oven, dropping temperature to 325 degrees. Bake 20–25 minutes or until internal bread temperature reaches 180 degrees.

Yield: 3 loaves

Breakfast Pilaf Bread

- 1 c. Kashi dry breakfast cereal blend
- 2 c. water
- 4 c. almond milk
- 3/4 c. honey
- 1-1/2 Tbsp. salt
- 2/3 c. canola oil
- 12 c. hard white wheat flour
- 4–6 c. high gluten bread flour
- 3 Tbsp. Saf-Instant® or other instant yeast

Cook Kashi, adding water, by conventional cooking method or by pressure cooker (20 minutes on low), natural release. Preheat oven to 400 degrees. Combine ingredients in Bosch bowl with dough hook, using only half of the flour, placing flour in last with yeast on top. Begin mixing, adding enough remaining flour until dough cleans sides of bowl (it may not require all of the flour). Knead 6 minutes or until gluten has developed. Remove from bowl and divide into loaves. Form loaves for pans or freestanding loaves. Let rise to double. Bake in preheated oven, dropping temperature to 325 degrees. Bake 20–25 minutes or until internal bread temperature reaches 180 degrees.

Yield: 6 loaves

Chef Brad tip

Placing instant yeast on top of the flour prevents killing the yeast.

English Scones

- 6 c. spelt white flour
- 1/2 c. sugar
- 1-1/2 Tbsp. salt
- 4 Tbsp. Rumford or other baking powder
- 1 c. butter (2 sticks), cold, cubed
- 3 eggs
- 1-1/2 c. milk

Mix all dry ingredients together and cut in butter. Mix all liquids together and combine with dry ingredients. Mix just to combine and form soft dough. Do no overmix. Place on counter and knead lightly for about 30 seconds. Overmixing and kneading will make scones tough. Roll out and cut with 2-inch biscuit cutter. Place on parchment-lined cookie sheet. Bake in preheated oven at 340 degrees for 10–12 minutes or until golden brown.

Yield: 3 doz.

Chef Brad tip

Try adding dry or frozen fruit, currants, or raisins to your dough.

Potato Flake Bread

- 1/2 c. instant potato flakes
- 3 c. warm milk
- 1/2 c. unsalted butter (1 stick), warm
- 2 Tbsp. sugar
- 2 eggs
- 3 tsp. salt
- 6–7 c. high gluten bread flour
- 3 tsp. Saf-Instant® or other instant yeast

Preheat oven to 400 degrees. Combine ingredients in Bosch bowl with dough hook, using only half of the flour, placing flour in last with yeast on top. Begin mixing, adding enough remaining flour until dough cleans sides of bowl (it may not require all of the flour). Knead 6 minutes or until gluten has developed. Remove from bowl and divide into loaves. Form loaves for pans or freestanding loaves. Let rise to double. Bake in preheated oven, dropping temperature to 325 degrees. Bake 20–25 minutes or until internal bread temperature reaches 180 degrees.

Yield: 3 loaves

Chef Brad tip

The true test of any bread is what kind of toast it makes.

Pullman Grain Bread

6 c. hot water (110 degrees)
3/4 c. shortening, melted
3/4 c. sugar
2 Tbsp. salt
4 c. spelt flour
2 c. teff, whole grain
10–12 c. high gluten bread flour
3 Tbsp. Saf-Instant® or other instant yeast

Preheat oven to 400 degrees. Combine ingredients in Bosch bowl with dough hook, using only half of the flour, placing flour in last with yeast on top. Begin mixing, adding enough remaining flour until dough cleans sides of bowl (it may not require all of the flour). Knead 6 minutes or until gluten has developed. Remove from bowl and divide into loaves. Form loaves for Pullman pans or freestanding loaves. Let rise to double. Bake in preheated oven, dropping temperature to 325 degrees. Bake 20–25 minutes or until internal bread temperature reaches 180 degrees.

Yield: 3 loaves

Chef Brad tip

Pullman pans are long, rectangular pans with a lid. Bread comes out shaped just like a square. Let dough rise and bake with the lid on.

Whole Wheat Bread Bowls

- 4 c. hot water (110 degrees) degrees)
- 2 Tbsp. salt
- 6 c. hard white wheat flour, freshly ground
- 2–4 c. high gluten bread flour
- 2 Tbsp. dough enhancer
- 3 Tbsp. barley malt
- 2 Tbsp. Saf-Instant® or other instant yeast
- Egg Wash (topping) (see page 57)

Mix thoroughly in Bosch bowl with dough hook. Continue adding whole wheat flour until mixture cleans sides of bowl. Knead on speed one for 6–8 minutes or until gluten is developed. Put lid on bowl and let dough sit for 15 minutes then, using the moment (or pulse) speed, knock dough down (dough hook should turn 5 revolutions). This procedure is called "pestering" the dough. Replace lid and repeat pestering procedure one more time. After pestering is completed, shape dough into 6 rounds and place on parchment-lined cookie sheet. Slash tops of dough with baker's blade and allow to rise until double in size. Brush with Egg Wash and bake in preheated 350 degrees oven for 25–30 minutes or until internal temperature reaches 210 degrees. Time will vary with ovens.

For use as a soup bowl, cut small piece off top and, using a fork, dig out the inside dough, being careful not to punch all the way through the sides or the bottom. Keep bread from the middle to make croutons. Fill bowl with a hearty soup and serve on a plate.

Yield: 6 soup bowls or 3 loaves

Olive Flat Bread

A wonderful bread—one of my all-time favorites! It's tasty and soul-satisfying as well.

- 1-1/2 c. hot water (110 degrees)
- 8 oz. feta cheese
- 2 Tbsp. olive oil, garlic flavored
- 2 tsp. salt
- 1-1/2 c. kalamata olives, chopped
- 1/2 c. buckwheat flour
- 1 c. soft wheat flour
- 2–3 cups high gluten bread flour
- 1 tsp. Saf-Instant® or other instant yeast

Preheat oven to 475 degrees. Combine ingredients in Bosch bowl with dough hook, using only half of the flour, placing flour in last with yeast on top. Begin mixing, adding enough remaining flour until dough cleans sides of bowl (it may not require all of the flour). Knead 6 minutes or until gluten has developed. Roll out like a pizza. Let rise for about 10 minutes. Bake on pizza stone for 5–7 minutes at 475 degrees.

Yield: 1 flat bread

Chef Brad tip

For low-fat bread, use 2 teaspoons lecithin granules to replace the 2/3 cup of oil.

14-Grain Bread

Healthful and tasty at the same time. I love it when that happens.

- 6 c. hot water (110 degrees)
- 2 c. 14-Grain Mix (recipe below), freshly ground
- 2–4 c. high gluten white flour
- 2/3 c. canola oil
- 2/3 c. honey
- 2 Tbsp. salt
- 3 Tbsp. dough enhancer
- 14 c. hard white wheat flour, freshly ground
- 3 Tbsp. Saf-Instant® or other instant yeast

Preheat oven to 400 degrees. Combine ingredients in Bosch bowl with dough hook, using only half of the flour, placing flour in last with yeast on top. Begin mixing, adding enough remaining flour until dough cleans sides of bowl (it may not require all of the flour). Knead 6 minutes or until gluten has developed. Remove from bowl and divide into loaves. Form loaves for pans or freestanding loaves. Let rise to double. Bake in preheated oven, dropping temperature to 325 degrees. Bake 20–25 minutes or until internal bread temperature reaches 180 degrees.

Yield: 5 loaves

14-Grain Mix:

- 6 c. 9-grain mix
- 1 c. amaranth
- 1 c. flax
- 1 c. sesame seeds
- 1 c. quinoa
- 1 c. millet

Rice Bread with Yeast

- 6-1/2 c. rice flour
- 5 tsp. xanthum gum
- 3 tsp. salt
- 1 c. dry milk powder
- 6 Tbsp. sugar
- 6 eggs
- 1/2 c. canola oil
- 3-1/2 c. water, plus
- 2 tsp. cider vinegar
- 4-1/2 tsp. Saf-Instant® or other instant yeast

Preheat oven to 400 degrees. Combine ingredients in Bosch bowl with dough hook, using only half the flour with yeast on top. Begin mixing, adding flour until dough cleans sides of bowl. Knead for 6 minutes to develop gluten. Divide into 2 loaves and let rise in loaf pans, sprayed with nonstick pan spray, until double in size. After placing bread in oven, drop temperature to 325 degrees. Bake 20–25 minutes or until internal bread temperature reaches 180 degrees.

Variations:

Cut out 1 cup of rice flour and replace with 2 cups popped amaranth* or 2 cups teff.

Yield: 2 loaves

*For instructions on popping amaranth, see page 7.

Chef Brad tip

Try baking freestanding loaves on a pizza stone.

Cranberry Breakfast Bread

You don't even have to be awake to make this one! This bread takes breakfast to a whole new dimension. It's wonderful and so easy.

1/2 c. cranberries
1 c. soft white wheat, freshly ground
2 c. high gluten bread flour
1/4 c. sugar
1/4 c. oil
1 c. hot water (110 degrees)
1 c. sourdough starter
1 Tbsp. salt
1 Tbsp. vanilla extract
3 Tbsp. Saf-Instant® or other instant yeast

Preheat pizza stone to 475 degrees. Add all ingredients, except the high gluten bread flour, to Bosch bowl with yeast on top. Begin mixing, adding high gluten bread flour until dough cleans sides of bowl. Knead 6 minutes. Roll out into round pizza shape then let rise for 20 minutes. Press finger holes in dough.

Topping:

Butter, melted
Sugar
Cinnamon
Maple syrup

Add topping and bake at 475 degrees for 5–7 minutes.

Yield: 1

Raisin Sourdough Bread

"2" Easy!

Sponge:

2 c. boiling water
2 c. raisins
2 c. sourdough starter
2 Tbsp. sugar
2 c. high gluten bread flour
2 Tbsp. Saf-Instant® or other instant yeast

In blender, blend raisins with boiling water for 1 minute on high. Pour blended raisins in Bosch bowl and add sourdough starter, sugar, and high gluten flour with yeast on top. Knead for 15–20 seconds. Let sponge rest for 15 minutes or longer.

Dough:

1 Tbsp. apple cider vinegar
1 Tbsp. salt
2 c. warm water
2/3 c. oil
2 Tbsp. dough enhancer
1/2 c. honey (or 1/3 c. fructose)
10–12 c. wheat or spelt, freshly ground

Preheat oven to 400 degrees. In bowl with sponge, add remaining ingredients, adding only half the flour called for. Begin mixing, adding flour until dough cleans sides of bowl. Knead for 6 minutes to develop gluten. Divide into loaves and let rise in loaf pans, sprayed with nonstick pan spray, until double in size. After placing bread in oven, drop temperature to 325 degrees. Bake 20–25 minutes or until internal bread temperature reaches 180 degrees.

Yield: 3 loaves

Spelt Bread

- 2 Tbsp. apple cider vinegar (optional)
- 5 c. hot milk (110 degrees)
- 1 Tbsp. salt
- 2/3 c. honey
- 2/3 c. oil
- 8–12 c. spelt flour, freshly ground
- 2 c. high gluten bread flour
- 3 Tbsp. Saf-Instant® or other instant yeast

Preheat oven to 400 degrees. Combine ingredients in Bosch bowl with dough hook, using only half of the flour, placing flour in last with yeast on top. Begin mixing, adding enough remaining flour until dough cleans sides of bowl (it may not require all of the flour). Knead 6 minutes or until gluten has developed. Remove from bowl and divide into loaves. Form loaves for pans or freestanding loaves. Let rise to double. Bake in preheated oven, dropping temperature to 325 degrees. Bake 20–25 minutes or until internal bread temperature reaches 180 degrees.

Yield: 4 loaves

Chef Brad tip

Most gluten-intolerant people who can't handle the gluten in wheat can handle spelt because it is a non-hybrid grain.

Spelt Sourdough Bread

The vinegar with the sourdough gives this bread an outstanding sourdough flavor.

- 4 Tbsp. apple cider vinegar (optional)
- 2/3 c. honey
- 2 c. sourdough starter
- 2/3 c. oil
- 2 Tbsp. salt
- 4 c. hot milk (110 degrees)
- 10–13 c. spelt flour, freshly ground
- 4 Tbsp. Saf-Instant® or other instant yeast

Preheat oven to 400 degrees. Combine ingredients in Bosch bowl with dough hook, using only half of the flour, placing flour in last with yeast on top. Begin mixing, adding enough remaining flour until dough cleans sides of bowl (it may not require all of the flour). Knead 6 minutes or until gluten has developed. Remove from bowl and divide into loaves. Form loaves for pans or freestanding loaves. Let rise to double. Bake in preheated oven, dropping temperature to 325 degrees. Bake 20–25 minutes or until internal bread temperature reaches 180 degrees.

Yield: 4 loaves

Chef Brad tip

Apple cider vinegar gives sourdough a more pronounced flavor. It is really a "cheater" method used to get great results.

Whole Wheat Sourdough Bread

- 4 c. hot water (110 degrees)
- 2/3 c. oil
- 1/3 c. honey
- 2 Tbsp. salt
- 3 Tbsp. dough enhancer
- 2 c. sourdough starter
- 10–13 c. hard white wheat flour
- 3 Tbsp. Saf-Instant® or other instant yeast

Preheat oven to 400 degrees. Combine ingredients in Bosch bowl with dough hook, using only half of the flour, placing flour in last with yeast on top. Begin mixing, adding enough remaining flour until dough cleans sides of bowl (it may not require all of the flour). Knead 6 minutes or until gluten has developed. Remove from bowl and divide into loaves. Form loaves for pans or freestanding loaves. Let rise to double. Bake in preheated oven, dropping temperature to 325 degrees. Bake 20–25 minutes or until internal bread temperature reaches 180 degrees.

Yield: 4 loaves

Chef Brad tip

Wipe pans with an oiled rag while hot and you won't have to wash them!

San Francisco Style Sourdough Bread

Light, nice, and perfect with a bowl of soup.

1-1/2 c. hot water (110 degrees)
1 c. sourdough starter
1 Tbsp. honey
2 tsp. salt
3–4 c. high gluten bread flour
1 Tbsp. Saf-Instant® or other instant yeast

Preheat pizza stone to 400 degrees. In Bosch bowl with dough hook, combine ingredients, using only half the flour with yeast on top. Begin mixing, adding flour until dough cleans sides of bowl. Knead for 6 minutes to develop gluten. Form into rounds. Cover and allow to rise until double in size. Make several slash lines in top of loaves with serrated knife. Place on parchment paper on cookie sheet. Bake on hot pizza stone for 40–45 minutes.

Yield: 3 small rounds

Chef Brad tip

For extra sour flavor add 2 tablespoons of apple cider vinegar.

Pumpkin Sourdough Bread

A wonderfully moist and tasty bread.

2 c. sourdough starter
2 c. pumpkin puree
4 c. hot water (110 degrees)
1 Tbsp. salt
2/3 c. oil
2/3 c. sugar
2 tsp. cloves, ground
1 Tbsp. ginger
2 Tbsp. cinnamon
1-1/2 c. pumpkin seeds
2 c. dried cranberries
2 Tbsp. dough enhancer
10 c. hard white wheat flour
2–4 c. high gluten bread flour
4 Tbsp. Saf-Instant® or other instant yeast

Preheat oven to 400 degrees. Combine ingredients in Bosch bowl with dough hook, using only half of the flour, placing flour in last with yeast on top. Begin mixing, adding enough remaining flour until dough cleans sides of bowl (it may not require all of the flour). Knead 6 minutes or until gluten has developed. Remove from bowl and divide into loaves. Form loaves for pans or freestanding loaves. Let rise to double. Bake in preheated oven, dropping temperature to 325 degrees. Bake 20–25 minutes or until internal bread temperature reaches 180 degrees.

Yield: 4 loaves

Sourdough White Bread

Sponging this bread really gives it extra texture and flavor.

Sponge:

2 c. sourdough starter
4 c. hot water (110 degrees)
4 Tbsp. sugar
6 c. high gluten bread flour
1 Tbsp. Saf-Instant® or other instant yeast

Mix ingredients in Bosch bowl and let set for 3-4 hours. Add the following ingredients:

1 c. hot water (110 degrees)
2/3 c. honey
2/3 c. oil
2 Tbsp. salt
2 Tbsp. apple cider vinegar
2 Tbsp. dough enhancer
6 c. high gluten bread flour
3 Tbsp. Saf-Instant® or other instant yeast

Preheat oven to 400 degrees. Combine ingredients in Bosch bowl with dough hook, using only half the flour with yeast on top. Begin mixing, adding flour until dough cleans sides of bowl. Knead for 6 minutes to develop gluten. Divide into loaves and let rise in loaf pans, sprayed with nonstick pan spray, until double in size. After placing bread in oven, drop temperature to 325 degrees. Bake 20–25 minutes or until internal bread temperature reaches 180 degrees.

Yield: 4 loaves

Pioneer Sourdough Bread

Before commercial yeast, bakers used starters to make bread rise. In southwestern ranches, lumber camps, and mining town kitchens, bubbling crocks of naturally fermenting sourdough starters were used to make pancakes, biscuits, and breads for every meal Since chuck wagon bakers on the trail often had no equipment, breads were mixed by making a well in the top of a sack of flour and adding the starter and salt to make a dough.

- 1-1/2 c. hot water (110 degrees)
- 1 Tbsp. sugar
- 1 c. sourdough starter or yogurt starter
- 1/2 c. butter, melted
- 1 Tbsp. salt
- 5-1/2 to 6 c. high gluten bread flour
- 1/4 c. fine yellow or white cornmeal (for sprinkling)
- 1 Tbsp. Saf-Instant® or other instant yeast

Preheat oven to 400 degrees. In Bosch bowl with dough hook, combine ingredients, using only half the flour with yeast on top. Begin mixing, adding flour until dough cleans sides of bowl. Knead for 6 minutes to develop gluten. Divide into loaves and let rise in loaf pans, sprayed with nonstick pan spray, until double in size. After placing bread in oven, drop temperature to 325 degrees. Bake 20–25 minutes or until internal bread temperature reaches 180 degrees.

Variations:

Add 1 or 2 cups raisins or dried blueberries, 1 cup granola, or 1 cup chopped pitted black olives to dough.

Yield: 2 loaves

Sourdough Blueberry Cherry Nut Bread

A sweet breakfast bread that braids well.

- 2-1/2 c. sourdough starter
- 5 c. hot water (110 degrees)
- 3/4 c. honey
- 2/3 c. canola oil
- 2 Tbsp. almond extract
- 2 Tbsp. salt
- 3 Tbsp. dough enhancer
- 1 c. dried blueberries
- 1 c. dried cherries
- 2–3 c. assorted nuts, chopped
- 6 c. hard white wheat flour, freshly ground
- 6–10 c. high gluten bread flour
- 3 Tbsp. Saf-Instant® or other instant yeast

Preheat oven to 400 degrees. In Bosch bowl with dough hook, combine ingredients, using only half the flour with yeast on top. Begin mixing, adding flour until dough cleans sides of bowl. Knead for 6 minutes to develop gluten. Divide into loaves and let rise in loaf pans, sprayed with nonstick pan spray, until double in size. After placing bread in oven, drop temperature to 325 degrees. Bake 20–25 minutes or until internal bread temperature reaches 180 degrees.

Yield: 5 loaves

Sourdough Light Caraway Rye Bread

- 1-1/2 c. whole grain rye, freshly ground
- 2 c. sourdough starter
- 2 c. hot water (110 degrees)
- 3 Tbsp. canola oil
- 1/3 c. barley malt syrup
- 1 Tbsp. salt
- 2 Tbsp. dough enhancer
- 3 Tbsp. caraway seeds
- 4–6 c. high gluten bread flour
- 2 Tbsp. Saf-Instant® or other instant yeast

Preheat oven to 400 degrees. In Bosch bowl with dough hook, combine ingredients, using only half the flour with yeast on top. Begin mixing, adding flour until dough cleans sides of bowl. Knead for 6 minutes to develop gluten. Form into 3 balls and place on parchment-lined cookie sheets. Cover and allow to rise until double in size. Slash several times with a serrated knife. Brush with beaten egg white. After placing bread in oven, drop temperature to 325 degrees. Bake 20–25 minutes or until internal bread temperature reaches 180 degrees.

Yield: 3 loaves

Chef Brad tip

Baking on parchment paper saves time and effort.

Sourdough Multi-Grain Dinner Rolls

I love this bread for the delightful textures the different grains add.

Sponge:

3 c. hot water
2 Tbsp. sugar
1 c. sourdough starter
3 c. high gluten bread flour
2 Tbsp. Saf-Instant® or other instant yeast

In Bosch bowl with dough hook, mix together all ingredients. Let rest for 20 minutes.

Dough:

3 eggs
1-1/2 sticks butter, cut in 1/4-inch chunks
1 Tbsp. salt
1/3 c. sugar
1/3 c. buckwheat, ground
1/3 c. Kamut®, ground
1/3 c. millet, ground
1/4 c. amaranth, popped*
6–8 c. high gluten bread flour

Add all ingredients to sponge and add high gluten flour as needed until dough starts to pull away from sides of the bowl. Remember to leave dough sticky when making dinner rolls. Knead for 6 minutes. After dough is kneaded, roll out 1/2-inch thick on floured counter and cut into long 2-inch strips. Brush with melted butter and stack six deep. Place in muffin tins and let rise. Bake at 350 degrees for about 20 minutes or until done.

Yield: 3 doz.

*For instructions on popping amaranth, see page 7.

Basic French Bread

Don't let the term "basic" fool you—this is a super bread.

- 1 Tbsp. sugar
- 2 c. hot water (110 degrees)
- 1 Tbsp. salt
- 3 c. high gluten bread flour
- 1-1/2 Tbsp. Saf-Instant® or other instant yeast
- Egg Wash (topping)
- Sesame seeds (topping)

Preheat oven to 400 degrees. In Bosch bowl with dough hook, combine ingredients with yeast on top. Begin mixing, adding flour until dough cleans sides of bowl. Knead for 6 minutes to develop gluten. Shape into long loaves. Brush with Egg Wash and sprinkle with sesame seeds. Let rise to double. After placing bread in oven, drop temperature to 325 degrees. Bake 20–25 minutes or until internal bread temperature reaches 210 degrees.

Yield: 2 loaves

Egg Wash:

- 1 egg
- 2 Tbsp. water

Beat together well.

Chef Brad tip

Spraying french bread with a spray bottle of water during baking will give the crust crispness.

Whole Wheat French Bread

There isn't enough whole wheat to make it 100 percent whole grain but enough to give it extra flavor and still retain the wonderful french bread texture.

2 c. hot water (110 degrees)
1 c. sourdough starter
2 Tbsp. oil
1 Tbsp. sugar
2 tsp. salt
2 c. hard white wheat flour
1–4 c. high gluten bread flour
2 Tbsp. Saf-Instant® or other instant yeast
Egg Wash (topping) (see page 57)
Sesame seeds (topping)

Preheat oven to 400 degrees. In Bosch bowl with dough hook, combine ingredients, using only half the flour with yeast on top. Begin mixing, adding flour until dough cleans sides of bowl. Knead for 6 minutes to develop gluten. Divide into 2 portions. Roll and shape into long loaves. Brush with Egg Wash and sprinkle with sesame seeds. Let rise to double. After placing bread in oven, drop temperature to 325 degrees. Bake 20–25 minutes or until internal bread temperature reaches 180 degrees.

Yield: 3 loaves

Old-World French Bread

This absolutely wonderful bread is the result of many attempts to combine bread and cheese together for a perfect meal.

2/3 c. scalded milk
2 Tbsp. butter, room temp.
2 tsp. salt
2 Tbsp. sugar
1 c. sourdough starter
1-1/3 c. water
4–6 c. high gluten bread flour
1 Tbsp. Saf-Instant® or other instant yeast
Egg Wash (topping) (see page 57)

Preheat oven to 400 degrees. In Bosch bowl with dough hook, combine ingredients except high gluten flour with yeast on top. Begin mixing, adding flour until dough cleans sides of bowl. Knead for 6 minutes to develop gluten. Divide dough. Form into long loaves, french bread style, and place in pans. Cover and let rise until double. Brush with Egg Wash. After placing bread in oven, drop temperature to 325 degrees and bake 20–25 minutes or until internal bread temperature reaches 180 degrees.

Variation:

Replace 2/3 cup scalded milk and 1-1/3 cup water with 2 cups water and 3 tablespoons powdered milk. Replace butter with 2 tablespoons lard.

Filling:

24 oz. cream cheese
1 c. feta cheese
2 Tbsp. pizza seasoning
2 Tbsp. olive oil
2 crushed garlic cloves

Combine ingredients and mix. Divide dough into portions. Roll out long and wide. Spread filling over dough.

Yield: 2 loaves

Whole Wheat & Quinoa French Style Bread

- 1 Tbsp. sugar
- 2 c. hot water (110 degrees)
- 3–6 c. high gluten bread flour
- 1 c. hard white wheat flour
- 1 Tbsp. salt
- 1 c. quinoa flour high gluten flour
- 1-1/2 Tbsp. Saf-Instant® or other instant yeast
- Egg Wash (topping) (see page 57)
- Sesame seeds (topping)

Preheat oven to 400 degrees. Combine ingredients in Bosch bowl with dough hook with yeast on top. Begin mixing, adding high gluten flour until dough cleans sides of bowl. Knead for 6 minutes to develop gluten. Roll and shape into long loaves. Brush with Egg Wash and sprinkle with sesame seeds. Let rise to double. After placing bread in oven, drop temperature to 325 degrees. Bake 20–25 minutes or until internal bread temperature reaches 210 degrees.

Variation:

May substitute 1 cup freshly ground blue cornmeal for 1 cup quinoa.

Yield: 2 loaves

Sourdough Kalamata French Bread

- 1-1/2 c. hot water (110 degrees)
- 1/4 c. dry milk powder
- 1-1/2 Tbsp. shortening
- 2 tsp. salt
- 3 Tbsp. sugar
- 4–8 c. spelt white flour
- 1/2 c. kalamata olives, chopped
- 1 c. sourdough starter
- 1-1/2 Tbsp. Saf-Instant® or other instant yeast
- Egg Wash (topping) (see page 57)

Preheat oven to 400 degrees. In Bosch bowl with dough hook, combine ingredients, except spelt white flour, with yeast on top. Begin mixing, adding flour until dough cleans sides of bowl. Knead for 6 minutes to develop gluten. Form into loaves and let rise until double. Slash top of bread. Brush with Egg Wash. After placing bread in oven, drop temperature to 325 degrees and bake 20–25 minutes or internal bread temperature reaches 210 degrees.

Yield: 2 loaves

Chef Brad tip

Hanging a wet cloth on the inside of the oven door during baking will give breads an extra crisp crust.

Multi-Grain French Bread

I love the buckwheat! It adds a wonderful texture and look to the bread. The popped amaranth makes it perfect.

- 2/3 c. scalded milk
- 2 Tbsp. butter, room temperature
- 2 tsp. salt
- 2 Tbsp. sugar
- 1-1/3 c. water
- 1 c. sourdough starter (optional)
- 4–6 c. high gluten bread flour
- 1 c. buckwheat, ground
- 1 c. amaranth, popped*
- 1 Tbsp. Saf-Instant® or other instant yeast
- Egg Wash (see page 57)

Preheat oven to 400 degrees. In Bosch bowl with dough hook, combine ingredients except high gluten flour with yeast on top. Begin mixing, adding flour until dough cleans sides of bowl. Knead for 6 minutes to develop gluten. Form into loaf and place in pan. Cover and let rise until double. Brush with Egg Wash. After placing bread in oven, drop temperature to 325 degrees, and bake 20–25 minutes or until internal bread temperature reaches 210 degrees.

Yield: 2 loaves

*For instructions on popping amaranth, see page 7.

Basic Rolls

Jean Flake, Aunt Jean to me, shares this recipe taught to her by her mother. Bread making is something Jean loves to do, and she certainly does it to perfection. She is well known for her light, wonderful tasting rolls and bread. Enjoy!

- 1 c. milk
- 4 Tbsp. butter or oil
- 1/4 c. sugar
- 1 tsp. salt
- 1 egg
- 5–6 c. flour
- 1 Tbsp. yeast

Scald milk or use powdered milk mixed according to directions. Add butter, sugar, salt, and 2 cups of high gluten flour. Mix until smooth. Beat in egg and yeast. Add flour to make a soft dough. Knead until smooth and elastic. If using Bosch mixer, add flour until dough barely cleans bowl. Shape into rolls and place in greased pan, barely touching each other. Let rise until double in bulk. If you are kneading by hand, let dough come up once before shaping into rolls. Bake at 350 degrees for 20–25 minutes. Can be used for cinnamon rolls or crescent rolls.

Yield: 1 doz. rolls

For more information about ingredients and equipment, please check out Chef Brad's website, www.chefbrad.com, or email chef@chefbrad.com

Dilly Feather Rolls

Light and flavorful! Make sure to leave the dough a little sticky.

- 5 c. hard white wheat flour
- 1/2 c. honey
- 1/4 c. dry milk powder
- 4 c. hot water (110 degrees)
- 4 tsp. salt
- 2/3 c. canola oil
- 1 c. cottage cheese, room temp.
- 3 Tbsp. dill weed
- 1/4 c. dried onion flakes
- 4 eggs
- 8–12 c. high gluten bread flour
- 3 Tbsp. Saf-Instant® or other instant yeast

Preheat oven 400 degrees. In Bosch with dough hook, combine wheat flour, powdered milk, and yeast. Mix thoroughly then add water, oil, honey, cottage cheese, dill weed, and onion flakes. Mix thoroughly. Sponge until doubled. Add salt and eggs. Mix, adding high gluten flour until mixture just begins to clean sides of bowl. Knead for 6 minutes. Form into rolls. Cover and let rise. Bake at 325 degrees for 18–20 minutes. Bottom should be slightly golden.

Yield: 4 doz. rolls

Mango Butter Rolls

1 c. hot milk (110 degrees)
1 tsp. sugar
1 Tbsp. Saf® or other instant yeast
2 medium mangoes
1 egg
1 Tbsp. salt
6 to 6-1/2 c. high gluten bread flour
1/2 c. unsalted butter (1 stick) room temp., cut into small pieces

Preheat oven to 375 degrees. Sprinkle yeast and sugar over warm milk. Let stand until bubbly. Peel mangoes and puree in blender, straining in sieve to make 1 cup of puree. Add egg, mango puree, salt, and some flour to yeast mixture. Turn on Bosch, adding flour a little at a time. Add pieces of butter. When dough starts to pull away from sides of bowl, knead for 6 minutes. Form into rolls. Let rise and bake for 15–18 minutes at 375 degrees.

Yield: 2 doz.

Pizza Dough in a Bag

Great for campouts and kids! I came up with this recipe for scout camp and have used it with children ever since. It works great—no mess and wonderful results!

3 c. high gluten bread flour
2 Tbsp. sugar
2 tsp. salt
1 c. hot water (110 degrees)
2 Tbsp. Saf-Instant® or other instant yeast
2 Tbsp. olive oil

Preheat oven to 475 degrees. Place ingredients in closed plastic Zip-lock bag and knead by hand for 6–8 minutes. Let rise in bag until double. Remove and form into pizza. Bake on parchment paper at 475 degrees for 5–7 minutes or bake in Dutch oven for 5–7 minutes.

Yield: 2 pizzas

Chef Brad tip

For pizza dough use the above recipe but substitute 1 cup of cornmeal or semolina flour for 1 cup of flour.

Soft Pretzels

The teff and amaranth give these pretzels a wonderful new twist.

1-1/4 c. hot water (110 degrees)
1/2 c. amaranth, popped*
1/2 tsp. sugar
1/4 c. teff
3 to 4-1/2 c. high gluten bread flour
1 Tbsp. Saf-Instant® or other instant yeast
Coarse salt (topping)
Egg Wash (topping) (see page 57)

Preheat oven 475 degrees. Place water, yeast, amaranth, sugar, teff, and 2 cups high gluten flour in Bosch bowl. Turn on Bosch, adding flour until dough cleans sides of bowl. Form into sticks or pretzels and place on sheet pan lined with parchment paper. Brush with Egg Wash and sprinkle with coarse salt. Let rise until almost double in size and bake in preheated 475-degree oven for about 10 minutes or until golden brown.

Yield: 1 doz.

*For instructions on popping amaranth, see page 7.

Chef Brad tip

Egg wash works like glue in holding toppings on the outside of the bread and gives pretzels their shiny surface.

Croissant Dough

1-2/3 c. milk
1/4 c. sugar
1 Tbsp. salt
3 Tbsp. butter, softened
High gluten bread flour
3 tsp. Saf-Instant® or other instant yeast

Place all ingredients in Bosch with yeast on top. Add enough flour to clean sides of bowl, and mix for 6 minutes. Let rest 1 hour in refrigerator.

5 sticks butter for roll-in
1/3 c. flour for roll-in
Egg Wash (topping) (see page 57)

Cream together butter and flour for the roll-in until smooth. Spread on a pan and chill. Pull butter from cooler 10 minutes before rolling dough. Roll dough out into a rectangle, 13 x 18 inches. Place butter on one side of dough and fold other side over to cover butter. Roll back out to 13 x 18 inches and fold into a trifold. Chill for 30 minutes and repeat 2 more times. Chill overnight.

Roll dough into rectangle, 14 x 16 inches. Mark top and bottom every 4 inches. Connect marks the first corner to first mark (upper right corner). Second cut is corner to second mark (upper left corner). Cut into two strips lengthwise (7 inches). Make 1/4-inch cut in top of each croissant. Roll up, starting with top edge. Place on sheet pan lined with parchment paper. Brush on Egg Wash evenly, proof, and bake at 375 degrees until browned.

Pita Bread

2 c. hot water (110 degrees)
2 tsp. sugar
1 Tbsp. salt
1/2 c. hard white wheat flour
4-1/2 c. high gluten bread flour
2 Tbsp. Saf-Instant® or other instant yeast

Preheat pizza stone to 475 degrees. In Bosch bowl with dough hook, combine ingredients, using only half the high gluten flour with yeast on top. Begin mixing, adding flour until dough cleans sides of bowl. Knead for 6 minutes to develop gluten. Form golf-ball-size balls. Let dough rest 10 minutes. Roll out to 1/4-inch thick and let proof about 10–12 minutes. Bake directly on pizza stone or on parchment paper for 5–7 minutes, turning over halfway through baking time.

Yield: 1 doz.

Chef Brad tip

The secret to puffy pita bread is a hot pizza stone; the high temperature causes them to puff.

Basic Corn Bread

2 tsp. salt
2 tsp. Rumford or other baking powder
5 c. white, yellow, or blue cornmeal, freshly ground
1 tsp. baking soda
4 Tbsp. honey
4 large eggs
4 Tbsp. oil
4 c. buttermilk

Mix dry ingredients together. Mix wet ingredients together. Add the dry to the wet, stirring constantly until smooth. Pour into greased pans and bake at 425 degrees for 20–25 minutes. Allow less time for muffins.

Chef Brad tip

Always use an aluminum-free baking powder, such as Rumford baking powder.

Old-Fashioned Corn Bread

This recipe is based on childhood memories of hot corn bread, right out of the oven, with a crispy crust and tender center. Please use the popping corn and don't substitute the bacon grease.

- 2 Tbsp. bacon drippings
- 2 c. popping corn, freshly ground
- 2 c. high gluten bread flour
- 1/2 c. sugar
- 1 tsp. salt
- 2 Tbsp. Rumford or other baking powder
- 1/3 c. dry milk powder
- 2 c. water
- 2 eggs
- 1/2 c. canola oil

Mix all ingredients (except bacon drippings) in Bosch mixing bowl for 2 minutes. Place large cast-iron skillet in preheated 400-degree oven with bacon drippings. When skillet is very hot, remove from oven and pour in batter. Place back in oven and bake for about 15–20 minutes.

Chef Brad tip

Popcorn contains less starch than field corn and makes a better corn bread.

Pumpkin Corn Bread

- 1/2 c. quinoa, toasted*
- 1/2 c. amaranth, popped**
- 2 c. popcorn, ground
- 1 c. high gluten bread flour
- 1 tsp. Rumford or other baking powder
- 1/2 tsp. baking soda
- 1 tsp. salt
- 1 c. canned pumpkin puree
- 2 c. nonfat buttermilk
- 1/4 c. molasses
- 4 large egg whites
- 1 Tbsp. unsalted butter, melted

Preheat oven to 425 degrees and spray baking dish with nonstick pan spray, such as Vegelene. Combine all dry ingredients in large bowl. In another bowl combine all wet ingredients. Pour wet ingredients over dry and stir until just combined. Pour batter into baking dish and bake about 30 minutes until wooden toothpick comes out clean. Let cool on wire rack.

**To Toast Quinoa (Same for Millet)*: In medium hot pan lightly toast quinoa, shaking frequently, until golden brown and you smell the nice toasted grain aroma.

**For instructions on popping amaranth, see page 7.

Pumpkin Blue Corn Rye Bread

This is an adaptation of an earlyy colonial multi-grain loaf known as "rye 'n injun bread," using pureed fresh pumpkin for added color, moisture, and flavor. Use canned or fresh pumpkin. Use parched blue corn for a particularly nutty flavor.

1/2 c. parched blue corn, coarsely ground
1 c. water
1/3 c. molasses
5 Tbsp. unsalted butter
1/2 c. pumpkin puree
2-1/2 tsp. salt
Drop of honey
1 c. hot water (110 degrees)
3/4 c. medium rye flour
3/4 c. hard white wheat flour
4 to 4-1/2 c. high gluten bread flour
1-1/2 Tbsp. Saf-Instant® or other instant yeast
1/4 c. blue cornmeal (for dusting pans)

In medium saucepan combine cornmeal and water. Cook over medium heat until bubbly and thickened, stirring constantly with a whisk. Stir in molasses, butter, pumpkin, and salt. Stir until butter is melted. Remove from heat and let cool. Preheat oven to 400 degrees. Combine ingredients in Bosch bowl with dough hook, using only half of the flour, placing flour in last with yeast on top. Begin mixing, adding enough remaining flour until dough cleans sides of bowl (it may not require all of the flour). Knead 6 minutes or until gluten has developed. Remove from bowl and divide into loaves. Form loaves for pans or freestanding loaves. Let rise to double. Bake in preheated oven, dropping temperature to 325 degrees. Bake 20–25 minutes or until internal bread temperature reaches 180 degrees.

Yield: 2 loaves

Notes

Pizzas, Bagels, Focaccias, Flat Breads, & Tortillas

Pizza Dough

- 1 c. hot water (110 degrees)
- 1 Tbsp. salt
- 3 Tbsp. sugar
- 2 Tbsp. olive oil
- 1 c. semolina flour
- 3 tsp. Dough Easy
- 2 c. high gluten bread flour
- 2 Tbsp. Saf-Instant® or other instant yeast

Place all ingredients in Bosch bowl and add flour until dough pulls away from side of bowl. Mix for 2 minutes. For a better dough, let set 15–20 minutes.

Sourdough Pizza Dough: Add 1 c. sourdough starter to above recipe.

Parmesan Pizza Dough: Add 1/2 c. grated Parmesan cheese to above recipe.

Pesto Pizza Dough: Add 1/3 c. fresh pesto to above recipe.

Spicy Pizza Dough: Add 2–3 Tbsp. pizza seasoning to above recipe.

Roasted Garlic Pizza Dough: Add 2–4 Tbsp. roasted garlic to above recipe.

Cinnamon Pizza Dough: Add 2 Tbsp. more sugar, 2 tsp. cinnamon, and 1 egg to above recipe.

Yield: 2 pizzas

Secret Pizza Dough

Looks like the secret is out!

- 1 c. hot water (110 degrees)
- 3 Tbsp. sugar
- 2 Tbsp. olive oil, or other flavor
- 1 Tbsp. salt
- 3 c. high gluten bread flour
- 3 egg whites
- 1 c. sourdough starter
- 3 tsp. Dough Easy
- 2 Tbsp. Saf-Instant® or other instant yeast

Preheat oven to 475–500 degrees. In Bosch bowl with dough hook, combine ingredients, using only half the high gluten flour with yeast on top. Begin mixing, adding flour until dough cleans sides of bowl. Knead for 6 minutes to develop gluten. Place in oiled bowl, cover, and let rise for 30–45 minutes. Cut dough into thirds. Bake directly on hot pizza stone or on stone covered with parchment paper.

To make wonderful hard rolls, leave dough a little sticky in Bosch. Form into rolls and let rise until double. Bake at 350 degrees until dark golden brown. They will be hard on the outside and light on the inside.

Yield: 2 large pizzas

Multi-Grain Pizza Dough

Tender and delightful!

- 1-1/2 c. hot water (110 degrees)
- 4 Tbsp. honey
- 1 Tbsp. salt
- 4 Tbsp. olive oil
- 1 c. sourdough starter
- 1/4 c. Kamut®
- 1/4 c. millet
- 1/4 c. brown rice
- 1/4 c. quinoa
- 1 c. hard white wheat flour or spelt flour
- 2 c. high gluten bread flour
- 3 Tbsp. Saf-Instant® or other instant yeast

Preheat oven to 475–500 degrees. In Bosch bowl with dough hook, combine ingredients except high gluten flour with yeast on top. Begin mixing, adding high gluten flour until dough cleans sides of bowl. Knead for 6 minutes to develop gluten. Then let rest for a half hour before using. Bake directly on hot pizza stone or on stone covered with parchment paper.

Yield: 2 large pizzas

Chef Brad tip

The secret to a good pizza crust is a hot pizza stone. Each pizza comes out better and better—so feed the kids first and save the last one for yourself!

Deep-Dish Pizza, Chicago Style

Dough:

1 c. water
1 Tbsp. sugar
3-1/2 c. high gluten bread flour
1/2 c. teff
1 tsp. salt
1/4 c. vegetable oil
1/2 c. yellow cornmeal
4 tsp. Dough Easy
1-1/2 Tbsp. Saf-Instant® or other instant yeast

Topping:

1 – 28 oz. can Italian style plum tomatoes
1 tsp. dried basil
1 tsp. oregano
Salt to taste
1/4 lb. Italian sausage, casing removed
10 oz. mozzarella cheese, sliced thin
Olive oil

Prepare dough in Bosch. Let dough rise double in bulk. Turn out and punch down. Place in oiled deep-dish pizza pan and press until dough covers bottom of pan. Preheat oven to 475 degrees and prick dough with fork. Bake 4 minutes. Remove from oven and brush with olive oil. Lay slices of cheese over crust, not the border. Combine tomatoes, basil, oregano, and salt. Spoon tomato mixture over dough. Sprinkle Parmesan cheese over tomatoes and add Italian sausages. Drizzle with olive oil. Bake 5 minutes on bottom rack and 20–25 minutes on middle rack until crust is lightly brown and sausage is cooked through.

Yield: 1 pizza

Basic New York Water Bagels

2-1/4 c. water
2 Tbsp. canola oil
2 tsp. salt
3 to 6-2/3 c. high gluten bread flour
4 Tbsp. barley malt syrup
4 tsp. Saf-Instant® or other instant yeast
Egg Wash (topping) (see page 57)
Toppings

Preheat pizza stone to 400 degrees. In Bosch with dough hook, combine ingredients in order, using only half the flour with yeast on top. Begin mixing, adding flour until dough cleans sides of bowl. Knead for 6 minutes. Remove from bowl and divide into 16 equal pieces. Roll each piece into a ball and let rest briefly. Meanwhile, bring 1-1/2 gallons water to boil with 1/3 cup malt syrup. Take dough balls and push thumb through, twirling to get desired shape, 1- to 1-1/2-inch hole. Place on parchment paper and let rest for 5–10 minutes. Drop bagel into boiling water until it floats, about 30 seconds on each side. With slotted spoon retrieve from boiling water and place on parchment paper. Brush with Egg Wash and bake on pizza stone at 400 degrees for about 20 minutes or until internal temperature reaches 180 degrees.

Suggested Toppings:

Poppy seeds, sesame seeds, garlic salt, and onions.

Yield: 16 bagels

14-Grain Bagels

A great tasting way to include extra grains in your diet. Try this wonderful bagel out as a sandwich or toasted with strawberry cream cheese.

2-1/2 c. hot water (110 degrees)
2 Tbsp. oil
6 Tbsp. barley malt syrup
2 c. hard white wheat flour, freshly ground
2-1/2 tsp. salt
1/3 c. 14-grain mix*
3–4 c. high gluten bread flour
4 tsp. Saf-Instant® or other instant yeast
Egg Wash (topping) (see page 57)

Preheat pizza stone to 400 degrees. In Bosch bowl with dough hook, combine ingredients in order, using only half the flour with yeast on top. Begin mixing, adding flour until dough cleans sides of bowl. Knead for 6 minutes. Remove from bowl and divide into 16 equal pieces. Roll each piece into ball and let rest briefly. Meanwhile, bring 1-1/2 gallons water to boil with 1/3 cup malt syrup. Take dough balls and push thumb through, twirling to get desired shape of 1- to 1-1/2-inch hole. Place on parchment paper and let rest for 5–10 minutes. Drop into boiling water until it floats, about 30 seconds on each side. With slotted spoon, retrieve from boiling water and place on parchment paper. Brush with Egg Wash and bake on pizza stone at 400 degrees for about 20 minutes or until internal temperature reaches 180 degrees.

Yield: 16 bagels

*See page 43.

Blueberry Bran Bagels

2-1/4 c. water
2 Tbsp. canola oil
4 Tbsp. barley malt syrup
2-1/2 tsp. salt
2 c. bran
4-2/3 c. high gluten bread flour
2 Tbsp. Vital wheat gluten (optional)
1 Tbsp. blueberry extract
4 tsp. Saf-Instant® or other instant yeast
Egg Wash (topping) (see page 57)

Preheat pizza stone to 400 degrees. In Bosch bowl with dough hook, combine ingredients in order, using only half the high gluten flour with yeast on top. Begin mixing, adding flour until dough cleans sides of bowl. Knead for 6 minutes. Remove from bowl and divide into 16 equal pieces. Roll each piece into ball and let rest briefly. Meanwhile, bring 1-1/2 gallons water to boil with 1/3 cup malt syrup. Take dough balls and push thumb through, twirling to get desired shape of 1- to 1-1/2-inch hole. Place on parchment paper and let rest for 5–10 minutes. Drop into boiling water until it floats, about 30 seconds on each side. With slotted spoon, retrieve from boiling water and place on parchment paper. Brush with Egg Wash and bake on pizza stone at 400 degrees for about 20 minutes or until internal temperature reaches 180 degrees.

Yield: 16 bagels

Chef Brad tip

Barley malt syrup enhances the texture and flavor of bagels.

Multi-Grain Focaccia

1-1/2 c. hot water (110 degrees)
1 c. sourdough starter
3 Tbsp. sugar
1 Tbsp. salt
3 Tbsp. extra virgin olive oil
2 c. spelt, freshly ground
1/2 c. whole teff
1-2 c. high gluten spelt white flour
3 Tbsp. Saf-Instant® or other instant yeast
1/4 c. tomato powder (optional)

Place all ingredients, except the high gluten spelt white flour, in Bosch bowl with yeast on top. Turn on Bosch. Add high gluten spelt white flour until dough cleans sides of bowl. Take dough out. Let rise until double. Punch down, roll out, then place on parchment-lined paddle. Let rise. Punch finger holes in dough. Brush olive oil over dough until covered. Sprinkle with Parmesan cheese and dried rosemary. Bake on pizza stone at 500 degrees for 5 minutes or until golden brown.

Chef Brad tip

High gluten spelt white flour is a processed spelt flour available at your health food store. It is the white flour of the spelt grain.

Southwestern Sourdough Focaccia

1 c. sourdough starter
1-1/4 c. hot water (110 degrees)
2 Tbsp. sugar
3 Tbsp. olive oil
1 Tbsp. salt
1/4 c. black bean flour
1/4 c. teff, whole grain
1/2 c. (or more) amaranth, popped*
2 c. high gluten bread flour
1/2 c. black olives, chopped
1/2 c. sundried tomatoes, chopped
1 jalapeño pepper, chopped
1/2 small onion, chopped
Small can green chilies, chopped
1/2 c. feta cheese
3 Tbsp. Saf-Instant® or other instant yeast
Boyajian Toasted Chili Oil or other flavored oil
Kosher salt

In Bosch bowl with dough hook, combine all ingredients, except half of the high gluten flour with yeast on top. Begin mixing, adding flour until dough cleans sides of bowl. Knead for 6 minutes to develop gluten then turn dough out on semolina-covered surface. Roll out to pizza shape. Place on parchment paper and let rise. With fingers, press holes on surface of bread. Brush liberally with Boyajian Toasted Chili Oil and sprinkle with rosemary. Bake on preheated pizza stone at 475 degrees for 5–8 minutes. Remove from oven and sprinkle with kosher salt.

*For instructions on popping amaranth, see page 7.

Sundried Tomato Focaccia

1 Tbsp. olive oil
1/2 c. onion
1 Tbsp. garlic
1 c. hot water (110 degrees)
2 Tbsp. sugar
1 Tbsp. salt
1/2 tsp. white pepper
1 Tbsp. chopped herbs, your choice (e.g., basil, rosemary, thyme, and oregano)
1/4 c. sundried tomatoes, rehydrated and chopped
4–5 c. high gluten bread flour
1 c. sourdough starter (optional)
1 Tbsp. Saf-Instant® or other instant yeast
Kosher salt (topping)

Sauté onions and garlic in olive oil and cool. In Bosch bowl place water, sugar, salt, pepper, herbs, tomatoes, sourdough starter, and half the flour with yeast on top. Turn on Bosch, adding enough flour to clean sides of bowl. Knead 6 minutes. Roll dough out, let rise until double about 30 minutes. Add topping and bake in preheated 450-degree oven on pizza stone until browned. Remove from oven and sprinkle with kosher salt.

Topping:

1/4 c. olive oil
1/4 c. herbs, chopped
3/4 c. Parmesan cheese, grated
Sundried tomatoes, rehydrated

Roasted Garlic Focaccia

4–6 roasted garlic cloves, chopped
1 c. hot water (110 degrees)
2 Tbsp. olive oil
1 Tbsp. salt
2 Tbsp. sugar
1 c. semolina
2 c. high gluten bread flour
1 Tbsp. rosemary, dried
2 Tbsp. Saf-Instant® or other instant yeast
Kosher salt (topping)

Place all ingredients, except rosemary, in Bosch mixing bowl and turn on. Add extra flour until dough cleans sides of bowl. Mix 6 minutes. Roll out flat, brush with olive oil, and sprinkle with rosemary. Bake at 450 degrees on pizza stone for 6–8 minutes. Remove and sprinkle with kosher salt.

Chef Brad tip

Kosher salt is free of added ingredients, and the texture really adds to focaccia breads.

Flour Tortillas

5 c. high gluten bread flour
2/3 c. lard or butter
2 tsp. salt
2 c. warm water or buttermilk

Cut lard or butter into flour and salt in the Bosch bowl using cookie beaters. Change to dough hook and add water until dough pulls away from sides of bowl. Knead for 3 minutes. Divide into 12 small balls. Roll and cook in tortilla press or cast-iron skillet.

Yield: 1 doz.

Chef Brad tip

If you use regular white flour instead of high gluten bread flour, add 2 teaspoons Rumford or other baking powder.

Tortillas Con Chili

5 c. high gluten bread flour
2 tsp. salt
1/3 c. lard
2 c. hot water (110 degrees)
1/3 c. chili powder

Mix all ingredients in Bosch with dough hook. Divide into 12–15 equal parts. Let rest at least 30 minutes before baking in tortilla press.

Yield: 1 doz.

Spinach Con Queso

1 pkg. frozen spinach
1 white onion
2 cans green chilies
8 oz. Velvetta cheese
3 oz. milk

Sauté onions and chilies. Add spinach, cheese, and milk. Cook until smooth.

Multi-Grain Flour Tortillas

4 c. high gluten bread flour
1 c. amaranth, popped*
1/2 c. teff
2 tsp. salt
2/3 c. lard or vegetable shortening
2 c. hot water (110 degrees)

Cut shortening into flour, grains, and salt in Bosch bowl, using cookie beaters. Change to dough hook and add water until dough pulls away from sides of bowl. Knead for 3 minutes. Divide into small balls. Roll and cook in tortilla press or cast-iron skillet.

Yield: 1 doz.

*For instructions on popping amaranth, see page 7.

Chef Brad tip

Be careful not to overcook your tortillas. Overcooking changes them to dry crackers.

Muffins, Pastries, & Pancakes

Sourdough Biscuits

6 Tbsp. butter, chilled
1-1/2 c. high gluten bread flour
1/2 c. quinoa, toasted* and freshly ground
1 tsp. salt
1 Tbsp. Rumford or other baking powder
2/3–3/4 c. milk
1 c. sourdough starter

In Bosch bowl with whips, cut butter into sifted dry ingredients. Change to dough hook and add sourdough starter and milk. Mix slowly, adding milk until dough is formed. Be careful not to overmix. Remove from bowl and place on floured surface. Flour top and roll out to desired thickness. Bake at 375 degrees for 11 minutes.

Yield: 1 doz.

*For instructions on toasting quinoa, see page 72.

Chef Brad tip

Sourdough changes a great recipe into something fantastic and long remembered.

Sourdough English Muffins

- 2 c. sourdough starter
- 3/4 c. buttermilk
- 2-3/4 to 3 c. high gluten bread flour
- 6 Tbsp. yellow cornmeal
- 1 tsp. baking soda
- 1/4 tsp. salt

Mix together sourdough starter and buttermilk. Combine flour, 4 tablespoons of the cornmeal, soda, and salt and add to buttermilk mixture. Stir to combine, using hands when necessary. Turn onto lightly floured surface. Knead until smooth, adding more flour if necessary. Roll dough to 2/3-inch thickness. Cover and let rise a few minutes. Using a 3-inch cutter, cut muffins. Sprinkle sheet of waxed paper with remaining cornmeal. Cover and let rise until very light, about 45 minutes. Bake on medium hot, lightly greased griddle about 30 minutes, turning often. Cool and split. Toast and serve with butter.

Zucchini Muffins

I stole this recipe from my dear friend, Chef Mark Armitage. I changed it a little. Sorry, Chef Mark, but I think it's better now.

- 4 eggs
- 2-1/8 c. sugar
- 1-2/3 c. salad oil
- 1-1/4 tsp. vanilla extract
- 4-1/4 c. zucchini, shredded
- 1-3/4 c. high gluten bread flour
- 1 c. Kamut® flour
- 2 tsp. Rumford or other baking powder
- 1-1/4 tsp. salt
- 2 tsp. baking soda
- 1-1/3 Tbsp. cinnamon
- 1-1/3 c. nuts
- 1-1/3 c. raisins

In mixing bowl with whips, mix first 4 ingredients to a mayonnaise-like texture. Change attachment to dough hook and add remaining ingredients. Bake at 350 degrees for 20 minutes.

Yield: 2 doz.

Sourdough Sticky Buns

Sticky, gooey, and yummy!

Dough:

3 c. sourdough starter
4 c. hot water (110 degrees)
1/2 c. dry milk powder
4 eggs
2/3 c. oil
1 c. sugar
1 Tbsp. salt
2 Tbsp. Dough Easy*
2 Tbsp. cinnamon
10–12 c. high gluten bread flour
3 Tbsp. Saf-Instant® or other instant yeast

Filling:

2 c. sugar
2–4 Tbsp. cinnamon

Topping:

Butter, melted
Brown sugar
Pecans, chopped
Karo syrup
Pure maple syrup

Place all dough ingredients in Bosch bowl in order given, using only half the flour. Turn on mixer, adding remaining flour until dough cleans sides of bowl. Knead only 4 minutes. Turn on oiled surface and divide into two portions. Roll out one portion until about 1/4- to 1/3-inch thick. Sprinkle with cinnamon and sugar. Cut with pizza cutter into 2-inch squares.

Cover bottom of baking dish with melted butter, chopped nuts and brown sugar. Dip seasoned squares into melted butter and pack squares in pan. Repeat for other portion of dough. Let rise and bake in 350-degree preheated oven until golden brown or until internal bread temperature reaches 180 degrees. Remove from oven and let cool for 2 minutes before tipping pan upside down to remove buns. Drizzle top with pure maple syrup.

Yield: 2 doz.

*Dough Easy helps relax the dough, making it easier to roll out. Works well with pizza dough too.

Chef Brad tip

Overbaking cinnamon rolls dries out the dough. For chewy, gooey rolls, underbake just a little.

Cinnamon Rolls

Extra light!

6 c. milk, scalded
3/4 c. butter (1-1/2 sticks)
1-1/2 c. sugar
6 whole eggs, beaten
8 c. (to start with) high gluten bread flour
2 Tbsp. salt
1/4 c. Saf-Instant® or other instant yeast
Cinnamon (topping)
Sugar (topping)
Nuts (optional topping)

Cool scalded milk to 110 degrees. Add all ingredients to Bosch bowl and mix. Let set for 20 minutes then turn on mixer. Add flour until dough pulls away from sides of bowl. Knead for 6 minutes to develop gluten. Divide dough into 4 equal portions. Roll out 1/4-inch thick and brush with melted butter. Sprinkle entire surface with cinnamon and sugar, adding nuts, if desired. Splash with water. Roll and cut into 1/2-inch thick rolls. Place on sprayed pan, allowing space between each roll. Let rise until double and bake for 5 minutes at 400 degrees. Reduce temperature to 325 degrees and bake for an additional 12 minutes.

Maple Frosting:

3 c. powdered sugar
2 Tbsp. butter, melted
1 Tbsp. hot water
1 Tbsp. maple extract

Add melted butter and desired amount of maple extract to powdered sugar. Add enough hot water to give glaze a smooth consistency.

Yield: 4 doz. large rolls

Banffshire Butteries (Morning Rolls)

Edna Graham shares this recipe, along with one of her memories of Scotland. Butteries were eaten as a breakfast roll or a treat, enjoyed when heading home after a dance with a stop at the local bakery for a fresh, warm buttery just out of the oven ...mmmm.

2-1/4 c .flour
1 tsp. salt
1 level Tbsp. white sugar
2 Tbsp. Saf-Instant® or other instant yeast
1 c. hot water (110 degrees)
1/2 c. lard, melted
1/2 c. butter (1 stick), melted

Mix salt and flour together. Place yeast and sugar in warm bowl. Add water, melted fats, and flour mixture. Mix for 3 minutes. Dough will be very soft. Form into rolls and place a little apart on parchment-lined baking sheet. Let rise. Bake at 400 degrees for 5 minutes then reduce heat to 350 degrees for 15 minutes or until internal temperature reaches 180 degrees.

Yield: 2 doz.

Chef Brad tip

To have a light buttery, be careful not to overwork your dough.

Christmas Morning Chocolate Rolls

- 1-1/2 c. hot water (110 degrees)
- 4–5 c. high gluten bread flour
- 1 c. butter (2 sticks), cut in small pieces
- 1/2 c. cocoa powder
- 1 tsp. salt
- 2 eggs
- 1/2 c. sugar
- 5 tsp. Saf-Instant® or other instant yeast

Place all ingredients for dough in Bosch bowl. Begin mixing, adding high gluten flour until dough pulls away from sides of bowl. Knead for 6 minutes.

Filling:

- 6 Tbsp. butter, softened
- 4 Tbsp. (heaping) brown sugar, crumbled
- 3 tsp. cinnamon
- 1 c. dark burgundy chocolate, grated
- 1 c. walnuts, finely chopped

Combine sugar, cinnamon, chocolate, and finely chopped walnuts in bowl. Set aside. Do not add butter. Roll dough out on oiled surface to about 1/3-inch thickness. Spread with soft butter, sprinkle filling over butter, roll up, and cut into 1-1/4 inch rolls. Place in buttered baking pan and let rise until double in size. Bake for 5 minutes at 400 degrees. Drop temperature to 325 degrees for 12 more minutes. After baking, brush with melted butter, cool and top with Glaze.

Glaze:

- 4 Tbsp. butter
- 2 c. powdered sugar
- Whipping cream

Combine butter, powdered sugar, and enough whipping cream to make sugar creamy.

Yield: 2 doz.

Buttermilk Potato Rolls or Doughnuts

- 3/4 c. freshly cooked potatoes, riced
- 1/2 c. butter (1 stick)
- 2 c. buttermilk
- 7-1/2 c. high gluten bread flour
- 2 Tbsp. sugar
- 1 tsp. salt
- 2 eggs
- 2 Tbsp. Saf-Instant® or other instant yeast

Ingredients should all be at room temperature. Mix in Bosch bowl, adding flour until dough pulls away from sides of bowl. Knead briefly. Let set in oiled bowl until doubles in size. Roll dough out and cut into doughnuts with cutter. Let rest before frying in hot oil for about 3 minutes, turning once to cook other side. Remove from oil and let drain on rack. Spread glaze on top.

Glaze:

- 4 c. powdered sugar
- 2 tsp. vanilla extract
- Water

Combine powdered sugar, vanilla, and enough water to make syrup-like consistency

Yield: 2 doz.

Chef Brad tip

To avoid greasy doughnuts, use dough with less sugar. Let doughnuts rest before frying; this keeps dough from soaking up oil.

Mamie's Pie Crust

My great-grandmother was the best pie maker. Her secret was lard—a no-no nowadays, but for extra special pie crust, use lard for best results. She always did.

3 c. high gluten bread flour	1 c. lard
1 tsp. salt	3/4 c. cold water

In Bosch bowl with whip, combine first 3 ingredients. Mix to pea size. Change to dough hook and add water. Mix lightly. Be sure not to overmix.

Yield: 1 pie or 2 shells

Multi-Grain Pie Crust

Light, flaky, and crisp. One of my favorite treats growing up was homemade tarts. Simply roll out extra pie dough, cut circles with biscuit cutter, spoon your favorite jam on top, and bake at 350 degrees until golden brown and bubbly. (Try eating just one of these!)

2-1/2 c. high gluten bread flour
1 c. amaranth, popped*
1-1/2 c. lard
1 tsp. salt
3/4 c. ice water

In Bosch bowl using whips, combine flour, salt, and lard. Mix until pea size. Remove whips and replace with dough hook. Turn to speed one. Drizzle water until dough pulls together. Do not overknead. Roll out onto pastry cloth. Bake, using directions from your pie recipe.

Yield: 1 pie or 2 pie shells

*For instructions on popping amaranth, see page 7.

Chef Brad tip

Handle lightly—this is a tender dough, perfect for pot pies, fruit pies, tarts, or anything that needs a pie crust.

Two-Easy Pancakes

A great way for children to learn how to make pancakes.

2 eggs
2 Tbsp. oil
2 tsp. salt
1 Tbsp. Rumford or other baking powder
2 c. milk
2 c. high gluten bread flour

Mix all ingredients except baking powder. After well mixed, add baking powder, whisk lightly, and gently ladle onto medium hot skillet. Cook until top starts to bubble, then turn over and cook other side for about half a minute. Serve hot with butter and syrup.

Yield: 2 doz.

Syrup:

2 c. white sugar
1 c. water
1 Tbsp. maple extract
2 tsp. vanilla extract
Ultra Gel or other thickening agent

Combine ingredients and enough Ultra Gel or other thickening agent to thicken to your liking.

Chef Brad tip

Syrup's a funny thing. As it sops into the pancake, children will want more. The trick is to use a thick syrup that stands on top of the pancakes.

5-Grain Pancake Mix

- 6 c. wheat
- 1 c. barley
- 1 c. rye
- 1 c. oat groats
- 1 c. brown rice
- 4 c. dry milk powder
- 3 tsp. salt
- 1 c. Rumford or other baking powder

Mix grains together and grind into flour. Add remaining ingredients, mixing well. Store in freezer until needed.

Pancakes:

- 1 c. pancake mix (above recipe)
- 1 egg, lightly beaten, or egg powder
- 1/2–3/4 c. water
- 1/4 c. sugar
- 2 Tbsp. oil

Yield: 1 doz.

Chef Brad tip

Replace the egg in pancakes and waffles with 2 tablespoons soy flour and 2 tablespoons water.

Blender Pancakes

1-1/4 c. water
1 c. soft white wheat
1/4 c. dry milk powder or buttermilk powder
1 egg
2 Tbsp. oil
2 Tbsp. honey
1/2 tsp. salt
1 Tbsp. Rumford or other baking powder

In blender mix water, wheat, and dry milk. Blend on high for 3 minutes. Add egg, oil, honey, and salt. Blend 20 seconds more. Add baking powder then pulse-blend 3 times—just enough to mix. Mixture will foam and get very light. Cook on hot nonstick griddle.

Yield: 2 doz. silver-dollar size pancakes

Chef Brad tip

One of the good things about Ultra Gel is that it doesn't crystalize. Use it for thickening syrups.

Sourdough Teff Pancakes

1 c. sourdough starter
3/4 c. instant potato flakes
4 eggs
1/4 c. sugar
1/4 c. canola oil
1 tsp. salt
2 Tbsp. Rumford or other baking powder
2 c. milk
2 c. high gluten bread flour
1/2 c. whole teff

In Bosch with whip attachment, mix all ingredients. Cook on hot griddle. Serve with butter and real maple syrup. For a real treat, top off with fresh fried eggs.

Yield: 2 doz.

Chef Brad tip

Pancakes and waffles are the perfect way to add nutrition to breakfast.

Spelt Kamut® Pancakes

- 1 c. spelt flour, freshly ground
- 1 c. Kamut® flour, freshly ground
- 1 c. high gluten spelt white flour or other high gluten bread flour
- 3 fresh eggs, or substitute with egg powder
- 1/3 c. tofu drink mix
- 1/4 c. powdered butter
- 1/3 c. instant vanilla pudding mix
- 1/4 c. Rumford or other baking powder
- 1 tsp. salt
- 3 c. water

In Bosch bowl with wire whips, place all ingredients and mix until well blended. Cook on griddle or waffle iron.

Yield: 3 doz.

Chef Brad tip

The addition of vanilla pudding was first by accident but now I add it all the time. It really adds flavor and texture.

Multi-Grain Yeasted Buttermilk Waffles

- 1 Tbsp. Saf-Instant® or other instant yeast
- 2 Tbsp. sugar
- 4 c. buttermilk
- 3/4 c. unsalted butter, melted
- 2 tsp. salt
- 1/2 c. teff
- 1/2 c. amaranth
- 2-1/2 c. Kamut® flour
- 2-1/2 c. spelt flour
- 4 eggs, beaten
- 1-1/2 tsp. baking soda

The night before serving, begin waffle batter. In Bosch bowl combine yeast, sugar, buttermilk, butter, salt, grains, and flour. Use cookie whips to blend. Mix well. Place cover on Bosch and place in refrigerator overnight. Next day, when ready to serve, spray waffle iron with nonstick spray and heat up. Beat eggs and baking soda together. Whisk into batter until evenly incorporated. Ladle onto waffle iron.

Yield: 6 waffles

About Waffles:

For a tender waffle, cook on a lower temperature. For a crisp waffle, cook on a higher temperature. To serve all at once, place cooked waffles in an oven preheated to 250 degrees to keep them warm. To store waffles, cool on wire rack and place in plastic freezer bags. Freeze up to one month. Can exchange Kamut® and spelt for 5 cups of any flour.

For more information about ingredients and equipment, please check out Chef Brad's website, www.chefbrad.com, or email chef@chefbrad.com

Vanilla Crepes

2 Tbsp. butter, melted
1-1/2 c. milk
3 eggs
2/3 c. soft white wheat flour
1 tsp. vanilla extract
1/2 tsp. salt
1/8 tsp. cinnamon

Best if made in advance and refrigerated before cooking. Mix all ingredients with wire whisk. Spray nonstick skillet with skillet spray or cover with melted butter. Pour in 1/4 cup mixture, tilting pan to cover. Cook 1 minute or until top is set. Loosen with spatula, shaking pan to loosen. Put on wax paper. Repeat until all batter is cooked. Place paper between each crepe. Serve filled with fruit and yogurt.

Yield: 2 doz.

Hot Cross Buns

- 3-1/2 c. high gluten bread flour
- 1/2 tsp. salt
- 1/2 c. sugar
- 1/2 tsp. cinnamon, ground
- 1/2 tsp. nutmeg, freshly grated
- 2 eggs
- 1 c. milk, scalded
- 4 Tbsp. butter
- 1 Tbsp. Saf-Instant® or other instant yeast
- 1 c. dried fruit mix (optional)

Place scalded milk, salt, sugar, spices, eggs, and butter in Bosch bowl. Add flour last with yeast on top. Turn on Bosch, adding just enough flour to clean sides of bowl. Add dried fruit and mix for 6 minutes. Form into 16 even balls and place in greased round cake pan to rise. Just before baking, place a cross on top of each roll.

Crosses:

- 3 Tbsp. flour
- 2 Tbsp. water
- 2 Tbsp. oil

Mix flour, water, and oil together to form a paste. Place into piping bag and, using plain tip, pipe a cross onto each roll. Bake at 425 degrees for 10 minutes, then reduce temperature to 375 degrees and bake 10–15 minutes longer. Brush with Sugar Glaze while hot.

Sugar Glaze:

Dissolve sugar with water in saucepan and boil for 2–3 minutes.

Yield: 16

Notes

Cookies, Cakes, & Non-Yeasted Breads

Old-Time Sugar Cookies

2 c. sugar
2 eggs
1 c. butter (2 sticks)
1 c. shortening
5 to 5-1/2 c. spelt flour
1 tsp. cream of tartar
1 tsp. salt
1 tsp. soda
3 tsp. vanilla extract
1 tsp. cardamom seed, ground

Mix ingredients well. Roll to desired thickness. Cut and bake at 325 degrees.

Yield: 2 doz.

Chef Brad tip

For chewy, tender cookies, try underbaking. For crispy cookies, bake a little longer.

Rolled Barley & Carob Chip Cookies

- 2 c. all-purpose flour
- 1 tsp. baking soda
- 1 tsp. baking powder
- 1/2 tsp. salt
- 1 c. unsalted butter (2 sticks) room temp.
- 1 c. granulated sugar
- 1 c. dark brown sugar, packed
- 4 egg whites
- 1 Tbsp. Wonderslim Fat and Egg Substitute
- 1 tsp. vanilla extract
- 2 c. rolled barley
- 6 oz. carob chips
- 3/4 c. pecan halves, chopped

Preheat oven to 350 degrees. Line baking sheet with parchment paper. Sift flour, baking soda, salt, and baking powder together. Set aside. Cream butter and both sugars together. Add egg whites and egg substitute. Mix thoroughly. Stir in vanilla then flour mixture. Mix well. Add rolled barley, carob chips, and nuts, mixing well after each addition. Drop by teaspoons onto prepared baking sheets. Bake until golden brown, about 15 minutes.

Yield: 2 doz.

Chef Brad tip

I always bake one cookie first to see what happens. If it is too mushy, add a little flour; if it is too stiff, a little vanilla. It can save you from ruining a whole pan of cookies.

Multi-Grain Cranberry Cookies

1/3 c. rice
1/3 c. quinoa
1/3 c. millet
2 c. water

Bring to boil, cover, and simmer on low heat for approximately 20–30 minutes. Set aside. Can be made night before and stored in refrigerator until ready to use.

In Bosch bowl, mix:

1 c. butter (2 sticks)
1-1/2 c. fructose
1/2 c. barley malt syrup
4 egg whites
1 Tbsp. vanilla extract
3-1/2 c. spelt flour
1 tsp. salt
1 tsp. baking soda
1/2 tsp. cinnamon
3 c. of above cooked grains
1-1/2 c. cranberries, dried
2 c. pecans, chopped

Cream butter, fructose, and malt syrup, then blend in egg whites. Add dry ingredients: grains, flour, salt, soda, vanilla, cinnamon, cranberries, and pecans. Dough will be more like a batter. Scoop onto cookie sheet lined with parchment paper. Bake at 350 degrees for 6–8 minutes.

Yield: Approx. 4 doz. delicious cookies

Shortbread

Delightfully light and crispy.

1 c. butter (2 sticks)
1/2 c. sugar
1-1/2 c. high gluten bread flour
1/4 c. teff
3/4 c. amaranth, popped*

Cream butter and sugar. Add high gluten flour and mix well. Form into 1-inch balls. Dust balls with flour. Stamp immediately with warm, oiled stamp. Bake at 350 degrees for 15–20 minutes. Cookies will keep their shape better if, after pressing, they are refrigerated 20 minutes on cookie sheet before baking.

Yield: 1 doz.

*For instructions on popping amaranth, see page 7.

Chef Brad tip

For an extra special treat, try dipping this shortbread in dipping chocolate.

Old-Time Gingerbread

- 1 c. molasses
- 1 c. sugar
- 1 c. shortening, melted
- 1 c. boiling water
- 1 tsp. baking soda
- 1 c. barley flour
- 1 c. Kamut® flour
- 3 tsp. ginger
- 4 tsp. cinnamon
- 1/2 tsp. nutmeg
- 1 tsp. cloves
- 1 tsp. allspice

Mix all ingredients in Bosch. Bake at 325 degrees for about 40 minutes in greased pans.

Yield: 1 doz.

Chef Brad tip

Especially nice served with a warm cup of cocoa on a cold day or a cold cup of cherry soup on a hot day

Gingerbread Boys & Girls

5 c. high gluten bread flour
1 tsp. salt
2 tsp. ginger
1 c. butter (2 sticks), melted
1 c. sugar
1 c. molasses
1 tsp. soda
1/2 c. hot water

Sift flour, salt, and ginger. Set aside. Mix butter, molasses, and sugar. Mix water with soda. Add dry ingredients to butter mixture alternately with soda water. Mix well and chill for 2–3 hours before using. Roll 1/8-inch thick on floured surface. Cut out cookies. Bake 10–12 minutes at 350 degrees.

Yield: 2 doz.

Easy Icing:

1 c. powdered sugar
1/2 tsp. vanilla extract
1/4 tsp. salt
1 Tbsp. heavy cream

Mix together sugar, vanilla, and salt, adding cream until frosting holds shape.

Biscotti

This is a cookie made for dipping in your favorite hot beverage.

- 2-1/2 c. high gluten bread flour
- 1/2 c. quinoa, toasted*
- 1/2 c. amaranth, popped**
- 2 tsp. Rumford or other baking powder
- 1/2 tsp. salt
- 4 eggs, slightly beaten
- 1 c. sugar
- 1/2 c. butter, melted
- 2 tsp. vanilla extract
- 1-1/2 tsp. almond extract
- 3/4 c. blanched almonds, minced

Combine dry ingredients together. Combine wet ingredients together then add to dry ingredients, mixing well. Spread half the dough onto cookie sheet to form loaf, 12 x 3 x 1-1/2 inches. Repeat with remaining dough. Bake at 350 degrees for 20 minutes or until it starts to turn brown around edges. Cool 10 minutes. Cut across loaf into slices 1/2-inch thick. Lay cookies cut-side down on cookie sheet and bake for 12 minutes. Turn over and bake 5–10 minutes longer until dry and crisp.

Yield: 4 doz.

*For instructions on toasting quinoa, see page 72.

**For instructions on popping amaranth, see page 7.

Blueberry Coffee Cake

1/2 c. amaranth, popped*
2-1/4 c. Kamut® flour
1 c. sugar
1-1/3 Tbsp. Rumford or other baking powder
3/4 tsp. cinnamon
1/3 tsp. salt
1 c. buttermilk
1/3 c. canola oil
2 eggs, well beaten
1 tsp. vanilla extract

Preheat oven to 350 degrees. Lightly oil 8 x 8-inch pan. For batter, combine first 6 ingredients in medium bowl. Make a well in center. Combine buttermilk, oil, eggs, and vanilla. Add all at once to flour mixture. Stir until dry ingredients are moistened and liquid is evenly distributed. Pour batter into pan.

*For instructions on popping amaranth, see page 7.

Topping:

3 c. blueberries, fresh or frozen
1/4 c. sugar
3/4 tsp. cinnamon
1/4 c. pecans, chopped

For topping, spread blueberries over top of batter. Combine sugar and cinnamon. Spoon over blueberries. Sprinkle with nuts. Bake at 350 degrees for 40 minutes or until wooden pick inserted in center comes out clean.

An Easy Make-Over:

Nuts can often be reduced by more than 50 percent, cutting saturated fat by nearly half.

Citrus Teff Amaranth Seed Cake

1 c. amaranth, popped*
3 c. high gluten bread flour
2-1/2 c. sugar
2-1/2 tsp. Rumford or other baking powder
3/4 tsp. salt
1-1/2 c. unsalted butter (3 sticks), room temp.
7 large whole eggs, lightly beaten
1-1/2 tsp. vanilla extract
1/3 c. teff
1 c. milk
1/2 tsp. each: grated lemon, orange, and lime peels

In Bosch bowl with whip, cream butter and gradually add sugar. Gradually drizzle eggs into bowl. Beat in vanilla. Mix flour, amaranth, salt, and baking powder and add this mixture, alternating with milk. Beat in teff and citrus. Divide batter evenly between prepared pans (2 loaf pans or 1 bundt cake pan). Bake in preheated 350-degree oven for 30 minutes. Cool about 15 minutes then spread with lemon glaze.

*For instructions on popping amaranth, see page 7.

Lemon Glaze:

1-1/2 c. powdered sugar
3 Tbsp. lemon juice, freshly squeezed
2 tsp. teff, plus more for sprinkling

Place sugar in medium bowl, gradually adding lemon juice. Stir with fork until smooth, adding more juice if needed. Mixture should be slightly thick. Stir in teff seeds. May be made 3–4 hours ahead and kept tightly covered in refrigerator.

Applesauce Mason Jar Cake

3-1/2 c. multi-grain flour (Kamut®, soft white wheat, spelt, millet, rye, etc.)
2 tsp. baking soda
2 c. raisins
2 c. nuts
1 tsp. salt
2 tsp. cinnamon
1 tsp. cloves
2 c. white sugar or brown, packed
1 c. butter (2 sticks)
1 egg
2 c. thick applesauce

Sift a little of the flour over raisins and nuts. Resift remainder of flour with salt, baking soda, cinnamon, and cloves. Cream butter, adding sugar gradually until light. Beat in egg. Stir flour mixture gradually into butter mixture until batter is smooth. Add raisins, nuts, and applesauce. Fill jars barely over half full. As soon as it is through baking, place sterile lid and ring on hot jar. Bake in greased wide-mouth jar at 350 degrees for about 45 minutes.

Yield: 6–8

Chef Brad tip

Non-yeasted bread or any cake can be baked in a jar.

Orange Teff Seed Bread

- 3 eggs, beaten
- 2-1/4 c. sugar
- 1-1/2 c. vegetable oil
- 1-1/2 c. milk
- 3 c. flour
- 1-1/2 tsp. Rumford or other baking powder
- 1 tsp. salt
- 1-1/2 Tbsp. teff
- 1/2 c. amaranth, popped*
- 3 c. high gluten bread flour
- 2 tsp. almond extract
- 1/4 c. orange concentrate, thawed

Preheat oven to 400 degrees. Combine all wet ingredients in Bosch and mix well. Sift together all dry ingredients and add to wet ingredients. Mix well. Divide into greased and floured bread pans. Bake in preheated oven at 325 degrees for 30–45 minutes or until knife comes out clean. Cool about 10 minutes then apply glaze while warm.

Yield: 4 loaves

*For instructions on popping amaranth, see page 7.

Orange Glaze:

- 1/4 c. orange juice concentrate, thawed
- 3/4 c. powdered sugar
- 1/2 tsp. vanilla extract
- 1 tsp. almond extract

Banana Bread

The secret to this bread is to stir the milk, soda, and vinegar together. Use a large bowl; it really bubbles.

- 12 bananas, mashed
- 1-1/2 c. shortening
- 2 Tbsp. baking soda (added to sour milk)
- 3 c. sour milk or buttermilk
- 6 c. sugar
- 2-1/4 tsp. salt
- 3 c. high gluten bread flour
- 3 c. Kamut® flour
- 3 c. soft white wheat flour
- 3 c. nuts, chopped

Cream together bananas, shortening, sour milk (with soda), and sugar. Add flour, salt, and nuts. Bake in greased tins 1 hour at 350 degrees.

Yield: 12 small loaves or 6 large loaves

Chef Brad tip

To make sour milk, add 2 tablespoons of vinegar to 3 cups milk.

Miscellaneous

Grain Loaf

This is a wonderful change for a nutritious breakfast. If you love pancakes and hot cereals, you will love this one—it's a combination of both.

Breakfast Loaf:

2 c. millet
1 c. amaranth
5 c. water
1/2 tsp. salt
Ghee (use for browning) (see page 146)
Butter (topping)
Maple syrup (topping)

Place millet, amaranth, water, and salt in pressure cooker. Pressure cook 6 minutes on high. Let pressure drop, natural release. Line loaf pan with plastic wrap. Place cooked grains in loaf pan. Cool and refrigerate. Slice and brown in ghee. Top with butter and maple syrup.

Dinner Loaf:

2 c. millet
1/2 c. amaranth
5 c. water
1/2 c. teff
1 Tbsp. chicken or beef soup mix (optional)
1/4 c. onion, dried
1/4 c. red bell pepper, dried
1/4 c. carrot, dried
2 Tbsp. garlic oil
1 tsp. salt

Place all ingredients in pressure cooker then use same instructions as above.

For more information about ingredients and equipment, please check out Chef Brad's website, www.chefbrad.com, or email chef@chefbrad.com

Hot Potato Soup

Too simple! Don't try to dress it up; it's a classic just how it is.

2 cans evaporated milk
2 c. water
6 large potatoes, peeled and chopped
1/2 c. butter (1 stick)
1/2 onion, chopped
2 Tbsp. olive oil
1 c. white quinoa, cooked
Salt and pepper to taste

Sauté onion in pressure cooker. Add remaining ingredients and bring to a boil. Place lid on pressure cooker and pressure 6 minutes on high, quick release. Remove and enjoy with hot bread.

Chef Brad tip

Sometimes the simplest recipes are the tastiest.

Savory Stew

- 2 lb. stew meat
- 2 c. carrots, finely chopped
- 2 c. cauliflower, finely chopped
- 1 c. mushrooms, finely chopped
- 1 Tbsp. Spike
- 4 Tbsp. rosemary oil
- 2 Tbsp. black pepper oil
- 1 c. sliced dehydrated potatoes
- 2 tsp. salt
- 1/3 c. Ultra Gel or other thickening agent
- 6 c. water
- 1/4 c. quinoa
- 1/4 c. amaranth

Brown meat in pressure cooker then add Spike, 2 tablespoons rosemary oil, and 1 tablespoon pepper oil. Pressure cook for 25 minutes on high, natural release. Remove lid and add all other ingredients except thickening agent. Pressure for 6–8 minutes on high. Remove from heat. Add more water if necessary. Thicken with Ultra Gel or other thickener.

Chef Brad tip

Thin soups that are too thick with beef or chicken broth. It keeps them from losing flavor.

Chili

- 2 lb. ground beef, cooked and drained
- 1 onion, chopped
- 3 Tbsp. Worcestershire sauce
- 1 c. red quinoa or millet, uncooked
- 2 Tbsp. olive oil
- 1 – 32-oz. bottle Knudsen's Very Veggie Vegetable Cocktail or Spicy V8
- 1/3 c. chili powder
- 1 can diced green chilies, drained

Cook ground beef and drain. Sauté onion and green chilies in 2 tablespoons olive oil. Add all other ingredients and pressure for 6 minutes on high, natural release.

Chef Brad tip

Add beans to make a great chili bean soup. My choice would be anasazi beans.

Kamut® Chili

2 c. Kamut® (cook with 5 c. water)
2 Tbsp. dried onion
1 Tbsp. ham soup base
1 lb. ground beef
1 Tbsp. balsamic vinegar
1/4 c. chili powder
1 c. diced green chilies
16 oz. Knudsen's Very Veggie Vegetable Cocktail

In pressure cooker (recommend using at least a 5-liter size) add Kamut® (with water), onion, and ham soup base and pressure cook on high for 1 hour. Brown meat. Add remaining ingredients to Kamut® mixture. Mix well. Bring pressure to high and cook approximately 5 minutes, natural release.

Optional Meatless Method:

Add 1 cup of millet and additional 6 cups of water to Kamut®, onion, and ham soup base. Pressure cook according to above directions, leaving out ground beef. Continue following above recipe.

Cream of Quinoa & Cauliflower Soup

8 c. chicken broth
1-1/2 c. quinoa
1 tsp. garlic
1 c. cauliflower, chopped
2 carrots, grated
4 Tbsp. olive oil
1 Tbsp. dried onion
1/4 c. green chilies, chopped

Place all ingredients in pressure cooker and pressure cook for 10–12 minutes on high, quick release. Remove lid and place soup in blender and puree. Serve with dollop of sour cream and croutons. If too thick, add a little water to thin down.

Chef Brad tip

Hot soup and a wonderful bread make for a great gourmet meal.

Savory Grain Chicken Soup

- 1 whole chicken
- 9 c. water
- Garlic oil
- Chili oil
- Plum vinegar
- 1/2 c. Baby Basmati or any white rice
- 1/2 c. quinoa
- 1/4 c. teff
- 1/4 c. amaranth
- 1 whole onion, chopped
- 1 c. peppers, finely chopped
- 1 Tbsp. salt

Place chicken, water, and oils in pressure cooker. Pressure cook on high for 12–20 minutes, depending on size of chicken. Use natural release. Remove from heat and remove meat from bone. Place in broth. Add remaining ingredients and pressure cook 8–10 minutes on high. If too thick, add additional water.

Chef Brad tip

The true test of a great cook is the quality of the ingredients that he or she uses.

Minestrone Soup

1/4 c. fruity olive oil
3/4 c. onion, chopped
1 Tbsp. garlic, minced
1 c. celery including tops, chopped
1 c. potatoes, diced
1 c. cabbage, shredded
1 c. green beans, diced
1 c. fresh plum tomatoes, chopped
6 c. broth
2 c. navy beans, cooked
1 c. cooked macaroni
Salt and pepper
1/2 c. Parmesan cheese, grated
1/4 c. fresh parsley, chopped
1/2 c. millet
Salt and pepper to taste

In large pressure pan, heat olive oil, adding onion and garlic. Sauté until onions turn yellow and add cabbage, celery, potatoes, and green beans. Sauté, then add tomatoes, millet, and broth. Pressure cook for 12 minutes on high, natural release. Remove lid and add cooked beans and pasta. Salt and pepper to taste. Add Parmesan cheese and stir well, adding chopped parsley when served.

Summer, Winter, Spring, or Fall Soup

- 1/4 c. millet
- 1/4 c. quinoa
- 1/4 c. rice
- 1/4 c. cracked wheat
- 1 plantain banana, cut in pieces
- 2 carrots, finely chopped
- 1 c. cauliflower, finely chopped
- 1/2 c. celery, chopped
- 1 c. potatoes, finely chopped
- 2 garlic cloves, finely chopped
- 1 onion, finely chopped
- 10 c. chicken broth
- 1/2 c. basil or parsley, chopped

Combine grains and broth in pressure pan. Pressure for 5 minutes on high, natural release. Open and add remaining ingredients. Pressure for an additional 5 minutes. Top off with fresh sorrel.

Chef Brad tip

Plantain (platano) looks like an extra large banana. Green platanos, with their potato-like texture, work well in soups. Ripe platanos are excellent baked or sautéed.

Quinoa Teff Chicken Corn Soup

1 chicken
1 large onion, diced
8 black peppercorns
1 bay leaf
1/2 tsp. dried thyme
Pinch saffron threads (optional)
Salt
3/4 tsp. black pepper, freshly ground
2 c. corn kernels
2 c. noodles
1/4 c. teff
1/2 c. quinoa

Place chicken, onion, peppercorns, bay leaf, and thyme in pressure cooker and fill with water. Pressure cook on high for 15 minutes, natural release. Remove chicken from pressure cooker, strip meat from the bones, and cut into bite-size pieces. Remove thyme, bay leaf, and peppercorns from broth. Add saffron, salt, and pepper, and bring to a boil. Add chicken, corn, noodles, and grains. Pressure cook for 5 minutes on low.

Chef Brad tip

If a thicker soup is desired, add a little Ultra Gel to thicken it up.

Chilled Cherry Soup

This recipe makes my knees weak! It is rich and, oh, so "gourmet-ish!"

2 lb. cherries, pitted
6 c. hot water (110 degrees)
2 c. sugar
2 tsp. orange oil or orange flavoring
3/4 c. red wine
1 tsp. nutmeg
1/2 c. Ultra Gel or other thickening agent

Put pitted cherries and water into a large pot and bring to boil. Cook until cherries are tender. Remove cherries from liquid and add sugar, red wine, orange oil, and nutmeg. Boil for about 15 minutes then add Ultra Gel. Stir until thick, add cherries, and cool. Serve with a dollop of sour cream.

Chef Brad tip

Ultra Gel is a modified cornstarch. To me it is one of the miracle foods of our generation. It thickens instantly, hot or cold.

Oxtail Millet Soup

2 lb. oxtail, cut in chunks and trimmed
1/2 c. high gluten bread flour
2 Tbsp. olive oil
2 medium onions, chopped
1/3 c. sherry or apple juice
2 qt. beef broth
2 Tbsp. ketchup
1/2 c. millet
2 tsp. salt
1/4 tsp. pepper
Fresh parsley
2 carrots, chopped
2 stalks celery, chopped
4 whole cloves
4–5 sprigs fresh thyme
Bay leaf

Dredge oxtail in flour and brown in oil. Remove and fry onions until golden brown. Add sherry. Add flour and brown then add broth, ketchup, meat, and millet. Make a bouquet garni by placing following ingredients in cheesecloth and tying it shut: salt, pepper, parsley, carrots, celery, cloves, thyme, and bay leaf. Place in pressure cooker and cook for about 45 minutes on high, natural release. Remove bouquet garni before serving soup.

Chef Brad tip

A bouquet garni is a way to add the essence of herbs and spices to your food. You then take it out so it doesn't overpower.

Clam Chowder

Great with a nice french bread.

- 1 c. onions, finely chopped
- 1 c. celery, finely diced
- 2 c. potatoes, very finely diced
- 2 cans (6-1/2 oz. each), minced clams and juice
- 3/4 c. butter
- 3/4 c. high gluten bread flour
- 4 c. half & half
- 1-1/2 tsp. salt
- 1 Tbsp. black pepper
- 2 Tbsp. balsamic vinegar

Drain juice from clams and pour over vegetables into pressure cooker pan, adding enough water to barely cover vegetables. Pressure cook for 3 minutes on high, quick release. Meanwhile, melt butter, add flour, and blend. Cook, stirring constantly. Add cream and cook, stirring with wire whip until smooth and thick (this is important). Add undrained vegetables, clams, and vinegar, and heat through. Season to taste with salt and pepper.

Chef Brad tip

Change clam chowder to salmon chowder just by adding fresh salmon and a dash of dill.

Fresh Basil Pesto

2 c. fresh basil
2 Tbsp. pine nuts, roasted
1 Tbsp. fresh garlic
3/4 c. olive oil
1/2 c. Parmesan cheese, freshly grated
Salt and pepper to taste

Add all ingredients except olive oil to Bosch blender or food processor. Blend. When mixed, slowly add olive oil.

Southwestern Pesto:

Add following ingredients to above recipe:

3 scallions
2 bunches cilantro, chopped
3 Tbsp. walnuts, roasted
1 Tbsp. fresh garlic
2/3 c. (instead of 1/2 c.) Parmesan cheese, freshly grated

Chef Brad tip

For added flavor and zest try pesto in any pizza dough or french bread recipe.

Corn Pesto Chowder

2 c. whole dry field corn
1/2 c. high gluten bread flour
1/2 c. butter (1 stick)
1 pt. half & half
2 c. chicken stock
1 Tbsp. pesto

Pressure cook corn in 4 cups water for 1 hour on high, natural release. Blend in Bosch blender. In saucepan melt butter and add flour. Mix well and add half & half and chicken stock. Stir until well blended. Add pesto and corn puree. Simmer 10 minutes. Serve hot with potato rolls.

Chef Brad tip

Serve with a dollop of sour cream, and if you're extra creative, a dash of caviar.

Multi-Grain Granola

A family favorite for snacking or breakfast

Combine:

- 4 c. rolled oats
- 2 c. quinoa, toasted*
- 2 c. millet, toasted*
- 1 c. rolled wheat or barley, rolled
- 1-1/2 c. amaranth, popped**
- 1 c. almonds, sliced
- 2 c. pecans, chopped
- 1-1/2 c. pumpkin seeds
- 1 c. raw cashews, chopped
- 1 c. raw sunflower seeds
- 2 c. unsweetened coconut
- 2 c. raw sesame seeds
- Dried cranberries or raisins

In saucepan, heat:

- 1 c. canola oil
- 2-1/4 c. honey
- 2-3 tsp. vanilla extract
- 1-1/2 tsp. maple flavoring
- 1/2 tsp. nutmeg, freshly ground
- 3/4 tsp. cinnamon
- 1-1/2 tsp. salt

Pour warm mixture over oat mixture and stir until moistened with liquid. Spray large pan with Vegelene or other nonstick pan spray. Pour mixture in pan. Spread mixture evenly; do not overfill. Bake at 350 degrees for 10–15 minutes. Stir every 3 minutes until golden brown. Remove and cool. Store in tight container with lid.

Variation:

Add raisins the last 5 minutes of baking time.

*For instructions on toasting quinoa and millet, see page 72.

**For instructions on popping amaranth, see page 7.

Pioneer Hardtack

4 c. whole grain flour (your choice)
1 c. rolled oats
1/2 c. shortening or butter
1 tsp. salt
1 tsp. baking soda
2 c. buttermilk, yogurt, cream, or sweet milk

Place all ingredients into a large bowl and mix until it forms a ball. Divide dough into small portions and roll out on lightly floured surface as thin as you can—the thinner it is rolled out, the better it will taste. Cut out as desired and place on greased sheet pan or parchment paper. Bake in 275-degree oven, turning each cracker after 15 minutes. Bake until golden brown and edges start to brown lightly. Store in airtight container. Crackers will remain fresh as long as they are kept dry.

Optional Seasonings:

Sprinkle on top: salt, onion powder, cheese powder, bacon bits, herbs, or spices. Or, mix barbecue sauce into dough.

Multi-Grain Crackers:

Omit 2-1/4 cups flour from above recipe and add following grains:

1 c. Kamut®
1/2 c. amaranth, popped*
1/2 c. teff
1/4 c. quinoa

Bake at 275 degrees until golden brown, turning each cracker after 15 minutes.

*For instructions about popping amaranth, see page 7.

Rice Blend

- 2 Tbsp. ghee
- 1 Tbsp. cumin seed
- 1 tsp. whole cardamom
- 1/2 stick cinnamon
- 1 c. Baby Basmati or other white rice
- 1/4 c. teff
- 1/4 c. amaranth
- 1/4 c. quinoa
- 1/4 c. millet
- 4 c. water
- Bay leaf

Sauté seasonings in ghee. Add rinsed rice and grains. Bring to boil. Pressure cook for 8 minutes on low, natural release, or simmer, covered, on low heat for 15 minutes.

Chef Brad tip

Ghee is clarified butter and is a healthful alternative to oils. It can be found in health food stores.

Peach Pie

This is a true crowd pleaser!

2 egg yolks
2 Tbsp. high gluten bread flour
1 c. sugar
2 tsp. vanilla extract
1/3 c. butter, melted
Nutmeg, grated
Canned peaches, drained

Preheat oven to 400 degrees. Line pie pan with pie crust. Combine above ingredients, blending well. Pour mixture over canned or fresh peaches that have been placed cut-side up in pie shell. Grate fresh nutmeg over custard. Bake for 15 minutes at 400 degrees. Lower temperature to 325 degrees and bake additional 45 minutes.

Chef Brad tip

Use Mamie's Pie Crust (page 102) or for extra special use, Multi-Grain Pie Crust (page 103).

Cranberry Apple Bread Pudding

1/2 c. butter, melted (1 stick)
1 c. half & half
1-1/2 c. milk
1-1/2 c. sugar
2 large eggs, beaten
1 tsp. vanilla extract
1/2 tsp. nutmeg
2 c. fresh apples, chopped
1 c. cranberries
(or 3 c. blueberries, dried)
8 c. french bread, cubed

Spray baking pan with nonstick spray. Combine all ingredients. Mix until bread is moist. Spoon mixture into prepared pan. Pour water in bottom of pressure pan and place trivet in pan. Bring water to boil. Cover pudding with tin foil and place pan in pressure cooker. Cover and pressure cook on high for 15 minutes, natural release.

Chef Brad tip

Try 14-Grain Bread (page 43) instead of french bread for a wonderful pudding.

Rice Pudding

4 c. hot water (110 degrees)
2 c. short-grain rice
4 c. half & half cream
1/2 c. butter (1 stick), cut in pieces
1 c. raisins, plumped
1-1/2 tsp. salt
1/2 tsp. cinnamon
1/4 tsp. nutmeg
3/4 c. sugar

Rinse rice 3 or 4 times in cool water. Heat pressure pan. Melt butter and add rice to pan. Stir to coat rice with butter. Add 2 cups half & half, water, and salt. Stir to ensure that rice does not stick to bottom of tpan. Close lid and pressure on low for 9 minutes, quick release. Stir contents and add raisins, sugar, and remaining half & half. Close lid and pressure 1 minute, natural release. Season with cinnamon and nutmeg. Serve

Chef Brad tip

*Adding cardamom,
whole cinnamon, star anise,
whole cloves, and cumin seeds
during the cooling process
will change a plain rice pudding
into something decadent.*

Super Grain Salad

1 tsp. salt
1 c. quinoa
1 c. millet
1 c. white rice
6 c. water

Pressure cook for 6 minutes on high, natural release. Remove from pressure cooker and chill.

Dressing:

1/2 c. flax oil
1/2 c. balsamic vinegar
2 garlic cloves, minced
1 tsp. pepper

Cut up your choice of vegetables—small zucchini, tomatoes, etc. Toss with chilled grains and dressing. Top with roasted pine nuts. Serve cold.

Chef Brad tip

Try flax oil in any salad dressing.
It binds well to make
great creamy vinegar dressings.

Hot Grain Salad

- 1 tsp. salt
- 1/2 c. black quinoa
- 1/2 c. millet
- 1/2 c. white rice
- 3 c. water
- 1 Tbsp. chicken bouillon
- 1/2 red bell pepper, chopped
- 1/2 yellow bell pepper, chopped
- 1/2 orange bell pepper, chopped
- 1/2 large onion, chopped
- 3 garlic cloves, chopped
- 2 Tbsp. garlic oil
- 1 Tbsp. sesame oil
- Bragg liquid aminos
- Plum vinegar

Pressure cook for 6 minutes on high, natural release. Remove from pressure cooker and chill. In a wok, sauté garlic, onions, and bell peppers in garlic oil and sesame oil. Add cooked grains. Toss and cook. Splash with Bragg liquid aminos and plum vinegar. Serve hot.

Chef Brad tip

Black quinoa has a nuttier, crunchier flavor than regular quinoa. I also love the look it gives to this salad.

Breakfast Cheese Boat

A little extra work but well worth it!

Bread:

- 2 c. hot water (110 degrees)
- Pinch of sugar
- 2 tsp. Saf-Instant® or other instant yeast
- 2 tsp. salt
- 2 c. spelt or whole wheat flour
- 3–4 c. high gluten bread flour
- 1 Tbsp. olive oil

Preheat pizza stone to 450 degrees. In Bosch bowl with dough hook, combine ingredients, using only two cups of high gluten flour with yeast on top. Begin mixing, adding high gluten flour until dough cleans sides of bowl. Knead for 6 minutes to develop gluten. Remove from pan and place in lightly oiled clean bowl. Cover with plastic wrap. Let rise until double in size. Gently push down dough. On lightly floured surface, using sharp knife, cut dough into 8 equal pieces. Flatten each piece with lightly floured palm of your hand then cover with plastic wrap while preparing filling.

Filling:

- 6 oz. soft cream cheese (for (breakfast) or young goat cheese (for other meals), room temp.
- 2 oz. Muenster cheese, coarsely grated, or cream cheese
- 1/3 c. plain yogurt
- 8 eggs
- 8 thin slices ham or Canadian bacon
- Secret Sauce (optional) (see recipe on next page)

Place cheese and yogurt in bowl and blend together to smooth consistency. Work with one piece of dough at a time, leaving remaining dough covered with plastic wrap. With your hands or rolling pin, stretch and flatten dough into long oval, 5 x 3 inches, and no more than 1/4-inch thick. Place slice of ham and generous 1/8 cup of filling in center of the oval. Spread to within an inch of edges.

Roll edges over to make thick rim, pinching sides together to form a point at ends (bread should look boat shaped). Slide breads onto paddle and then onto pizza stone. Crack egg over top of each bread. Bake at 450 degrees until crust is golden and bottom is firm and crusty, about 12–15 minutes. Serve hot.

Secret Sauce:

- 1/4 c. balsamic vinegar
- 1/3 c. red wine vinegar
- 1/3 c. Barlean's flax oil
- 1/3 c. olive oil
- 1 Tbsp. pepper
- 1 Tbsp. salt
- 2 Tbsp. oregano, dried

Place all ingredients in blender and puree. Place in mustard squirt bottle. Shake before using.

Chef Brad tip

Secret Sauce is great for subway sandwiches, salads, and everything else that needs a little zip.

Lemonade Syrup

2 c. sugar
1 c. water
Rind of 2 lemons, cut into strips
1/8 tsp. salt
6 lemons, juiced

Boil sugar, water, and lemon rind for 5 minutes. Cool and add juice of lemons and salt. Strain syrup and store in covered container. To make, add 2 tablespoons to glass of ice water or soda.

Rebecca Sauce

1 pt. sour cream
1/3 c. brown sugar
1/4 c. milk
Dash of vanilla extract
Pinch of cinnamon or nutmeg

Whisk together ingredients until consistency of ranch dressing, adding more milk if necessary. Serve thick over fresh strawberries. Sprinkle with raisins.

Chef Brad tip

For a refreshing summertime treat, try fresh strawberries with Rebecca Sauce.

Hummus

- 4 c. garbanzo beans, cooked
- 3/4 c. lemon juice, freshly squeezed
- 3 cloves garlic, peeled
- 1 c. tahini
- 1 Tbsp. olive oil
- 1/4–1/2 c. cold water
- Salt
- Paprika (optional)

Place drained beans and 1/4 cup lemon juice in blender and process until beans are mashed but not completely pureed. Add garlic, 1/2 cup lemon juice, olive oil, and tahini and process until a smooth puree. Slowly add water to thin if mixture seems too thick. Season to taste with salt. Sprinkle with paprika before serving. Serve chilled or at room temperature.

Chef Brad tip

Hummus is a wonderful spread for any of these breads and crackers.

For more information about ingredients and equipment, please check out Chef Brad's website, www.chefbrad.com, or email chef@chefbrad.com

Notes

Index

A

Allergies/wheat sensitive 10,15,18,47
Amaranth 7,10,56,62,67, 72,85,90,103,109,110, 118,121,122,123,125,129, 131,135,144,145,146
  Popping 7
Applesauce Mason Jar Cake 124

B

Bagels
  Basic New York Water 81
  Blueberry Bran 83
  14-Grain 82
Barley Malt Syrup 51,81, 82,83
Banana Bread 126
Banffshire Butteries 99
Barley 7,8,15,30,41,105, 116,119,144
Basic Corn Bread 70
Basic New York Water Bagels 81
Basic French Bread 57
Basic Rolls 63
Basic Whole Wheat Bread 21
Beans 11,132
  Anaszi 132
  Black 36,85
  Garbanzo 155
  Navy 136
  Soybeans 30
Biscotti 121
Biscuits 17
  Sourdough 93
Black Bean Jalapeño Bread 36
Blender Pancakes 106
Blueberry Bran Bagels 83
Blueberry Coffee Cake 122
Bosch, about 3
Bouquet garni 140
Boyajian Toasted Chili Oil 85
Bran 83
Bread in a Bag 66
Breads 7-18,**19-73**
  Basic Corn Bread 70
  Basic French 57
  Basic Rolls 63
  Basic Whole Wheat 21
  Black Bean Jalapeño 36
  Breakfast 25
  Breakfast Pilaf 37
  Buttermilk Multi-Grain 30
  California Walnut 27
  Cranberry Breakfast 45
  Cracked Wheat Feather 28
  Cranberry Vanilla Seed 23
  Dilly Feather Rolls 64
  English Scones 38
  14-Grain 43
  Good Ol' White 22
  Grandma's Rye 24
  Herb 34
  Lemony Fennelly 33
  Mango Butter Rolls 65
  Multi-Grain French 62
  Old-Fashioned Corn 71
  Old-World French 59
  Olive Flat 42
  Pioneer Sourdough 53
  Pita 69
  Potato 35
  Potato Flake 39
  Pullman Grain 40
  Pumpkin Blue Corn Rye 73
  Pumpkin Corn 72
  Pumpkin Sourdough 51
  Raisin Rye 32
  Raisin Sourdough 46
  Rice Bread with Yeast 44
  San Francisco Style Sourdough 50
  Soft Pretzels 67
  Sourdough Blueberry Cherry Nut 54
  Sourdough Kalamata French 61
  Sourdough Light Caraway 55
  Sourdough Multi-Grain Dinner Rolls 56
  Sourdough White 52
  Spelt 47
  Spelt Sourdough 48
  Vienna 31
  Whole Wheat and Quinoa French Style 60
  Whole Wheat Bread Bowls 41
  Whole Wheat French 58
  Whole Wheat Sourdough 49
  Wild Rice Molasses 29
Breakfast Bread 25
Breakfast Cheese Boat 152
Breakfast Pilaf Bread 37
Bromine free 2
Buckwheat 8,10,42,56,62
Bulgur wheat 5
Buttermilk 26,30,33,34, 70,72,88,94,101,106, 109,122,126,145
Buttermilk Bread 26
Buttermilk Multi-Grain Bread 30
Buttermilk Potato Rolls or Doughnuts 101

C

Cakes 16,17
  Applesauce Mason Jar 124
  Blueberry Coffee 122
  Citrus Teff Amaranth Seed 123
California Walnut Bread 27
Caviar 143
Cereals 8,9,11,13,28,129
Chili 132
  Kamut® 133
Chilled Cherry Soup 139
Christmas Morning Chocolate Rolls 100
Cinnamon Pizza Dough 77
Cinnamon Rolls 98
Citrus Teff Amaranth Seed Cake 123
Clam Chowder 141
Clams 141
Coconut 23, 144
Cookies 7,11,12,14,16,115
  Biscotti 121
  Multi-Grain Cranberry 117
  Gingerbread Boys & Girls 120
  Old-Time Gingerbread 119
  Old-Time Sugar 115
  Rolled Barley & Carob Chip 116
  Shortbread 118
Cookies,Cakes, & Non-Yeasted Breads 113-126

Corn bread 12
Basic 70
Old-Fashioned 71
Pumpkin 72
Pumpkin Blue Corn Rye 73
Corn Pesto Chowder 143
Couscous 9
Cracked Wheat Feather Bread 28
Crackers
Mult-Grain 145
Pioneer Hardtack 145
Cranberry Apple Bread Pudding 148
Cranberry Breakfast Bread 45
Cranberry Seed Mixture 23
Cranberry Vanilla Seed Bread 23
Cream of Quinoa & Cauliflower Soup 134
Crepes, Vanilla 110
Croissant Dough 68

D-E-F

Deep-Dish Pizza, Chicago Style 80
Dilly Feather Rolls 64
Doughnuts
Buttermilk Potato 101
Egg Wash 57,67
English Muffins Sourdough 94
English Scones 38
5-Grain Pancake Mix 105
Flake, Jean 63
Flour Tortillas 88
Focaccias
Multi-Grain 84
Roasted Garlic 87
Southwestern Sourdough 85
Sundried Tomato 86
14-Grain Bagels 82
14-Grain Bread 43,148
14-Grain Mix 43,82
French Breads 142,148
Basic 57
Multi-Grain 62
Old-World 59
Sourdough
Kalamata 61
Whole Wheat & Quinoa French Style 60
Whole Wheat 58
Fresh Basil Pesto 142
Fructose 46,117
Fruits 38
Apples 148
Applesauce 124
Banana, plantain 137
Blueberries 54,122,148
Cherries 54,139
Cranberries 45,117,144, 148
Currants 38
Lemon 33,123,154,155
Lime 123
Mangoes 65
Olives
Black 85
Kalamata 42,61
Orange 123,125
Peaches 147
Raisins 38,46,95,144, 149
Strawberries 154

G

Ghee, about 146
Gingerbread Boys & Girls 120
Glaze 100,101
Lemon 123
Orange 125
Sugar 111
Good Ol' White Bread 22
Graham, Edna 99
Grain Loaf 129
Grandma's Rye Bread 24
Granola 53
Multi-Grain Granola 144

H-K

Herb Bread 34
High gluten spelt white flour 61,84,108
Hot Cross Buns 111
Hot Grain Salad 151
Hot Potato Soup 130
Hummus 155
Italian sausage 81
Kamut® 9,10,56,79,95, 108,109,119,122,124, 126,133,145
Kamut®, Chili 133
Kasha 8,10
Kashi dry breakfast cereal blend 37
Knudsen's Very Veggie Vegetable Cocktail 132, 133
Kosher salt, about 87

L

Lecithin granules 42
Lemonade Syrup 154
Lemony Fennelly Bread 33
Maize (see Corn)
Mamie's Pie Crust 102
Mango Butter Rolls 65
Maple Frosting 98
Millet 10,11,15,16,43,56,79, 117,124,129,132,133,136, 137,140,144,146,150,151
Toasting 72
Minestrone Soup 136
Miscellaneous 127-155
Muffins 16
Sourdough English 94
Zucchini 95
Muffins, Pastries, & Pancakes 91–111
Multi-Grain Cranberry Cookies 117
Multi-Grain Flour Tortillas 90
Multi-Grain Focaccia 84
Multi-Grain French Bread 62
Multi-Grain Granola 144
Multi-Grain Pie Crust 103
Multi-Grain Pizza Dough 79
Multi-Grain Yeasted Buttermilk Waffles 109
Mushrooms 131

N-O

9-grain mix 30,43
9-grain cracked cereal mix 30
Nuts 54,95,98,125
Almonds 23,121,144
Pecans 96,116,117,122, 144
Pine 142
Walnuts 27,100,142
Oats 11,12,16,144,145
Bran 12
Groats 11,28,105
Oatmeal 11,12
Old-fashioned 11
Quick 11
Rolled 11,144,145,
Old-Fashioned Corn Bread 71
Old-Time Gingerbread 119
Old-Time Sugar Cookies 115
Old-World French Bread 59
Olive Flat Bread 42
Orange Teff Seed Bread 125
Oxtail Millet Soup 140

P

Pancakes 8-17,107
  Blender 106
  Five-Grain Pancake Mix 105
  Sourdough Teff 107
  Spelt Kamut® 108
  Two-Easy 104
Parmesan Pizza Dough 77
Pastries 7,10,14,17
  Banffshire Butteries 99
  Buttermilk Potato Rolls or Doughnuts 101
  Christmas Morning Chocolate Rolls 100
  Cinnamon Rolls 98
  Hot Cross Buns 111
  Sourdough Sticky Buns 96
Peach Pie 147
Pesto 142,143
  Fresh Basil 142
  Southwestern 142
Pesto Pizza Dough 77
Pestering 41
Pie crust
  Mamie's 102
  Multi-Grain 103
Pilaf 8
Pioneer Hardtack 145
Pioneer Sourdough Bread 53
Pita Bread 69
Pizza Dough 77
  Secret 78
  Cinnamon 77
  Deep-Dish, Chicago Style 80
  Multi-Grain 79
  Parmesan 77
  Pesto 77
  Pizza Dough in a Bag 66
  Roasted Garlic 77
  Sourdough, 77
  Spicy 77
Pizzas, Bagels, Focaccias, Flat Breads, & Tortillas 75–90
Potato Bread 35
Potato Flake Bread 39
Pretzels, soft 67
Puddings
  Cranberry Apple Bread 148
  Rice 149
Pullman Grain Bread 40
Pumpkin Blue Corn Rye Bread 73
Pumpkin Corn Bread 72
Pumpkin Sourdough Bread 51

Q

Quinoa 10,12,13,43,60,72, 79,93,117,121,130,131, 132,134,135,137,138, 144,145,146,150,151
  Black 151
  Red 132
  Toasting 72
Quinoa Teff Chicken Corn Soup 138

R

Raisin Rye Bread 32
Raisin Sourdough Bread 46
Rebecca Sauce 154
Rice 13,14,16,44,117,137
  Baby Basmati 13,135, 146
  Brown 13,14,79,105
  Short grain 149
  White 14,149,150,151
  Wild 29
Rice Blend 146
Rice Bread with Yeast 44
Rice Pudding 149
Roasted Garlic Focaccia 87
Roasted Garlic Pizza Dough 77
Rolled Barley & Carob Chip Cookies 116
Rolls 26,32,78
  Basic 63
  Buttermilk Potato 101
  Dilly Feather 64
  Mango Butter 65
  Sourdough Multi-Grain 56
Rye 14,24,32,55,73,105, 124
Rye bread
  Raisin 32
  Grandma's 24
  Sourdough Light Caraway 55

S

Salads 7,8,10,11,16,153
  Hot Grain 151
  Super Grain 150
Salmon chowder 141
San Francisco-Style Sourdough Bread 50
Savory Grain Chicken Soup 135
Savory Stew 131
Scones, English 38
Secret Pizza Dough 78
Secret Sauce 152,153
Seeds
  Caraway 14,24,32,55
  Cardamom 115,146,149
  Cumin 146,149
  Flax 23,43
  Poppy 81
  Pumpkin 23,51,144
  Sesame 23,43,57,58,60, 81,144
  Star Anise 149
  Sunflower 25,43,144
Semolina 8,66,77,85,87
Shortbread 118
Side dishes 8,9,10,11,13,16
Sneak nutrition 1
Soft Pretzels 67
Soups 7,8,10,11,13,17,50, 131,137
  Chilled Cherry 139
  Clam Chowder 141
  Corn Pesto Chowder 143
  Cream of Quinoa & Cauliflower 134
  Hot Potato 130
  Minestrone 136
  Oxtail Millet 140
  Quinoa Teff Chicken Corn 138
  Savory Grain Chicken 135
  Summer, Winter, Spring, or Fall 137
Sourdough 36,45,46,48, 49,50,51,52,53,54,55,56, 58,59,61,62,77,78,79,84, 85,86,93,94,96,107
  Sourdough Biscuits 93
  Sourdough Blueberry Cherry Nut Bread 54
  Sourdough Kalamata French Bread 61
  Sourdough English Muffins 94
  Sourdough Light Caraway Rye Bread 55
  Sourdough Multi-Grain Dinner Rolls 56
  Sourdough Pizza Dough 77
  Sourdough Sticky Buns 96
  Sourdough Teff Pancakes 107
  Sourdough White Bread 52
Southwestern Pesto 142
Southwestern Sourdough Focaccia 85
Soybeans 15,30,105

Spelt 15,16,24,31,38,40, 46,47,48,61,79,84,108, 109,113,115,117,124, 152
  High gluten spelt white flour 61,84,108
Spelt Kamut® Pancakes 108
Spelt Bread 47
Spelt Sourdough Bread 48
Spicy Pizza Dough 77
Spinach Con Queso 89
Stews
  Savory Stew 131
  Summer, Winter, Spring, or Fall Soup 137
Sundried Tomato Focaccia 86
Super Grain Salad 150
Syrup 104

T

Tahini 155
Teff 16,40,44,67,80,84, 85,90,107,109,118,123, 125,129,135,138,145,146
Those Wonderful Grains! 5-18
Tortillas Con Chili 89
Tortillas 9
  Flour 88
  Multi-Grain Flour 90
  Con Chili 89
Triticale 16,17,18
Two-Easy Pancakes 104

U-V

Vanilla Crepes 110
Vegetables
  Cabbage 136
  Carrot 129,131,134,137, 140
  Cauliflower 131,134,137
  Celery 137,140,141
  Cilantro 142
  Corn 36,73,138
    Cornmeal 53,60,66, 70,73,80,94
    Dent 9
    Field 9,12,71,143
    Popping/popcorn 11, 12,28,71,72
    Whole kernel 36,138
  Garlic 34,59,86,87,136, 137,142,151,155
  Green beans 135,136
  Green chilies 85,89,132, 133,134
  Onion 35,85,86,129,132, 135,136,137,140,141, 151
  Parsley 137
  Peppers 135
    Bell 151
    Jalapeño 36,85
    Red 129
  Potatoes 35,130,131,135, 136,137,141
    Flakes 39, 107
  Pumpkins 51,72,73
  Scallions 142
  Spinach 89
  Tomatoes
    Plum 135,136
    Sundried 85,86
  Zucchini 95
Very Veggie Vegetable Cocktail, Knudsen's 132,133
Vienna Bread 31

W-X-Y-Z

Waffles 10,12,13,15,17,107
  Multi-Grain Yeasted Buttermilk 109
Wheat, about 7,8,10,15,16, 17,18
  Bulgur, about 8
  Cracked, about 18
  Durum 9,17,18
  Flakes, about 18
  Hard red, about 17
  Hard white, about 17
  Soft, about 17,18
Whole Wheat and Quinoa French Style Bread 60
Whole Wheat Bread Bowls 41
Whole Wheat French Bread 58
Whole Wheat Sourdough Bread 49
Wild Rice Molasses Bread 29
Wonderslim Fat and Egg Substitute 116
Xanthun gum 44
Zucchini Muffins 95